CHRISTMAS
DOT MARKERS ACTIVITY BOOK

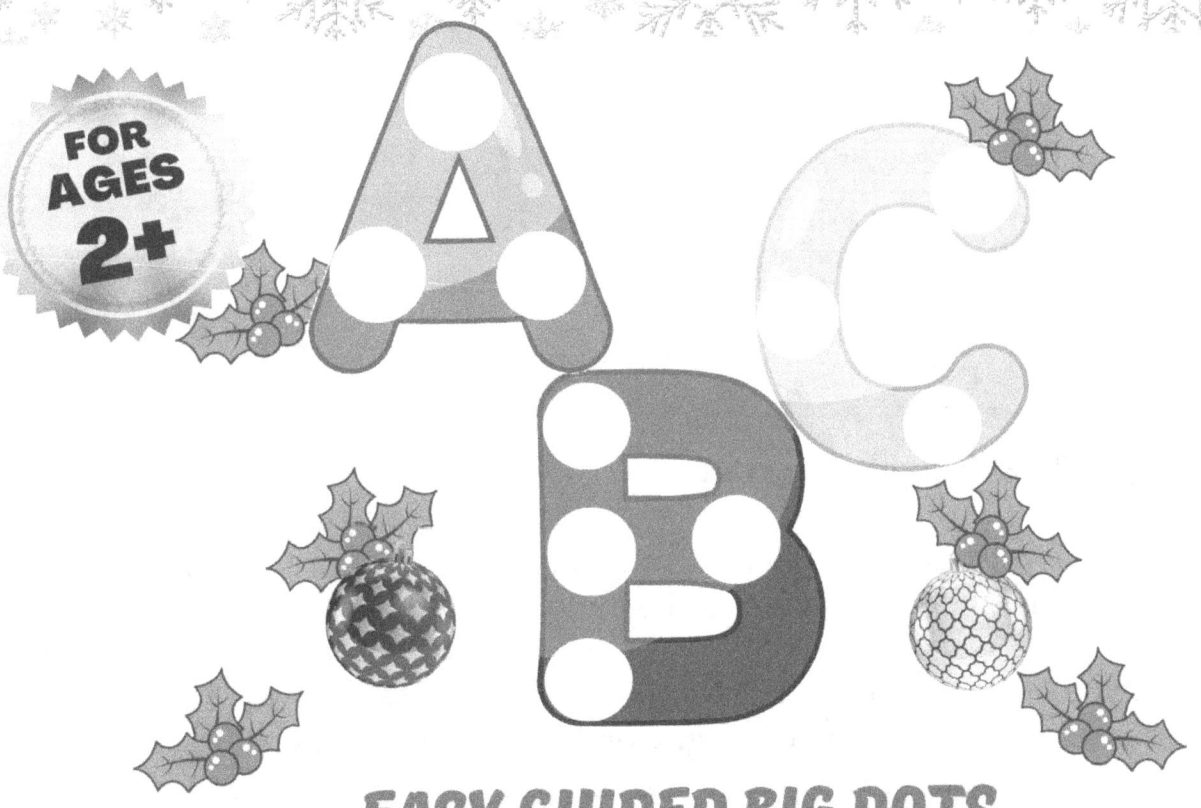

FOR AGES 2+

EASY GUIDED BIG DOTS

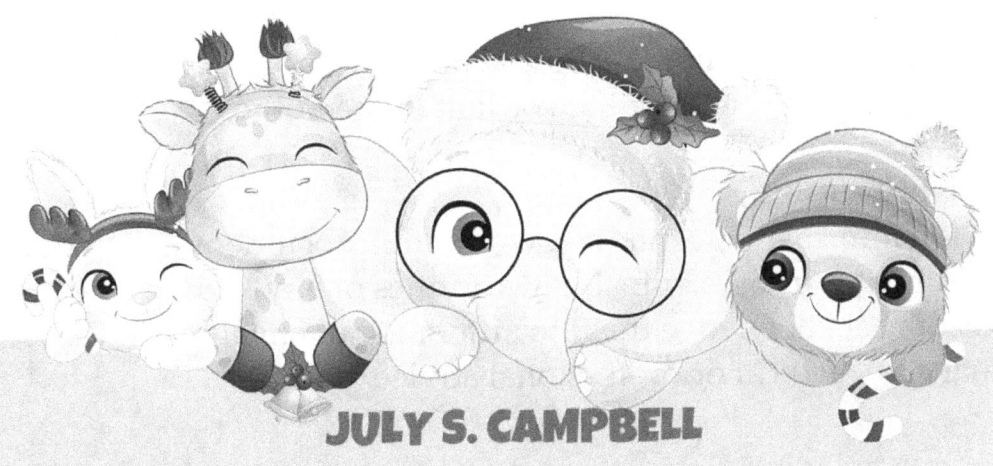

JULY S. CAMPBELL

© **Copyright 2020 - All rights reserved.**

The contents of this book may not be reproduced, duplicated or transmitted without direct written permission from the author.

Under no circumstances will any legal responsibility or blame be held against the publisher for any reparation, damages, or monetary loss due to the information herein, either directly or indirectly.

Legal Notice:
You cannot amend, distribute, sell, use, quote or paraphrase any part of the content within this book without the consent of the author.

Disclaimer Notice:
Please note the information contained within this document is for educational and entertainment purposes only. No warranties of any kind are expressed or implied. Readers acknowledge that the author is not engaging in the rendering of legal, financial, medical or professional advice.

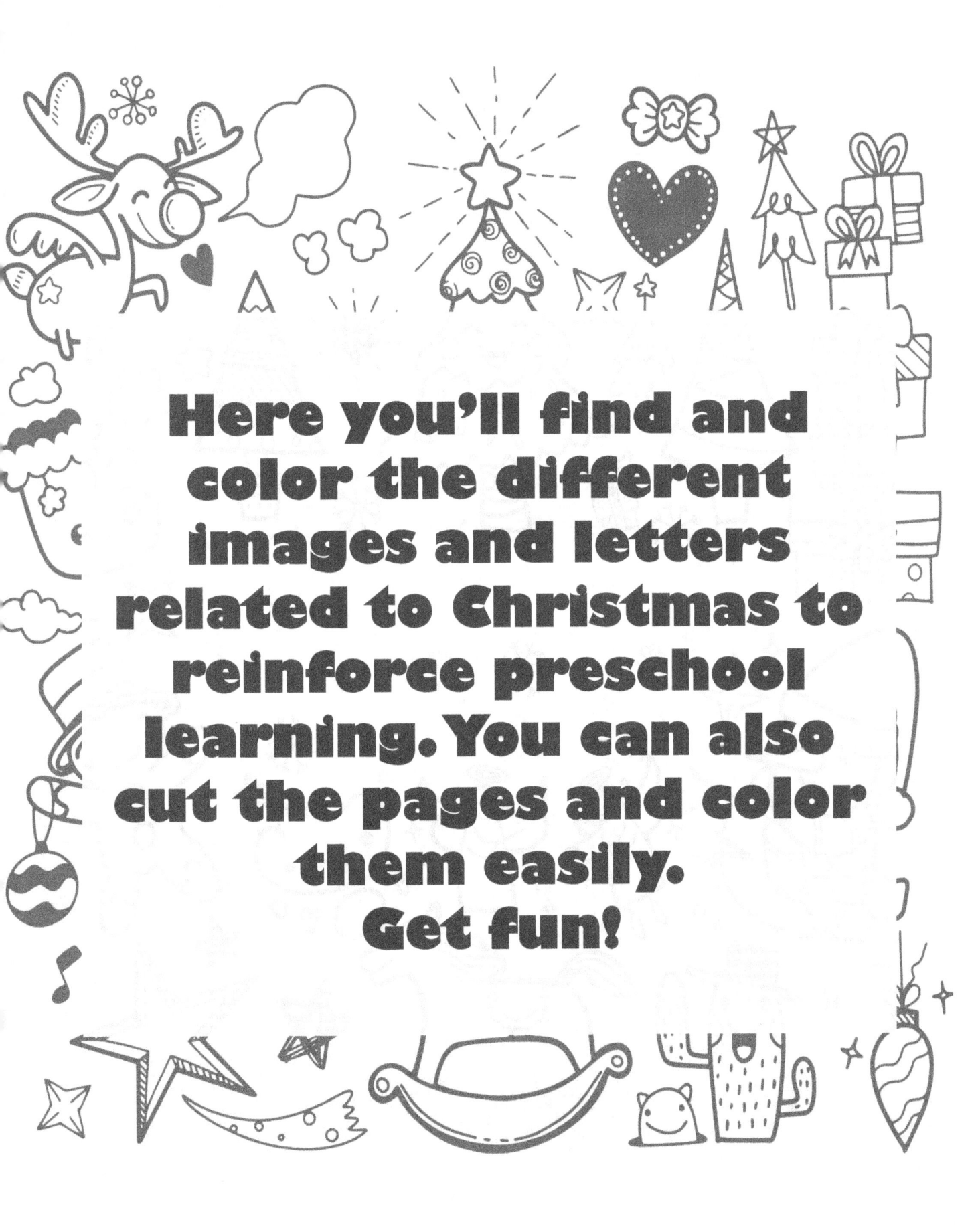

Here you'll find and color the different images and letters related to Christmas to reinforce preschool learning. You can also cut the pages and color them easily.
Get fun!

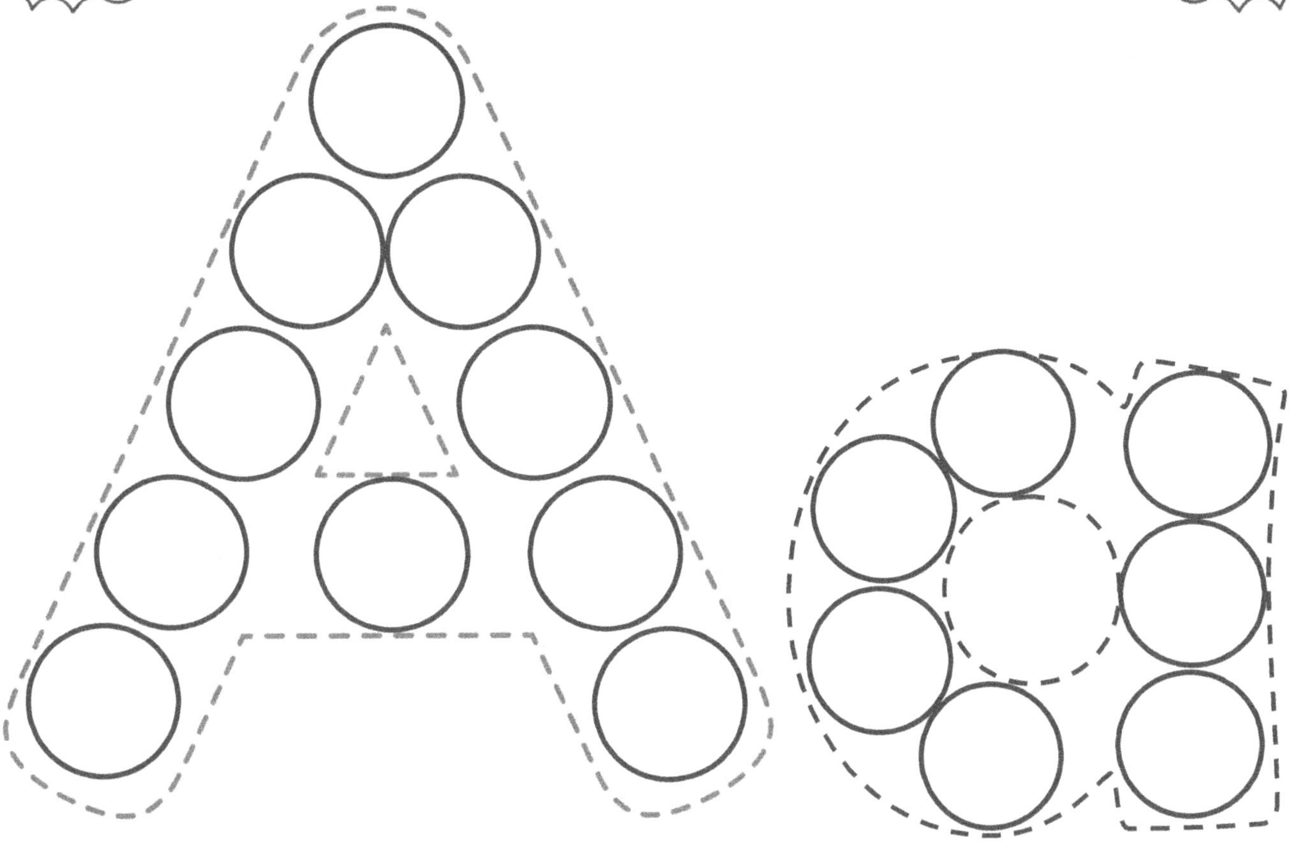

A is for alpaca

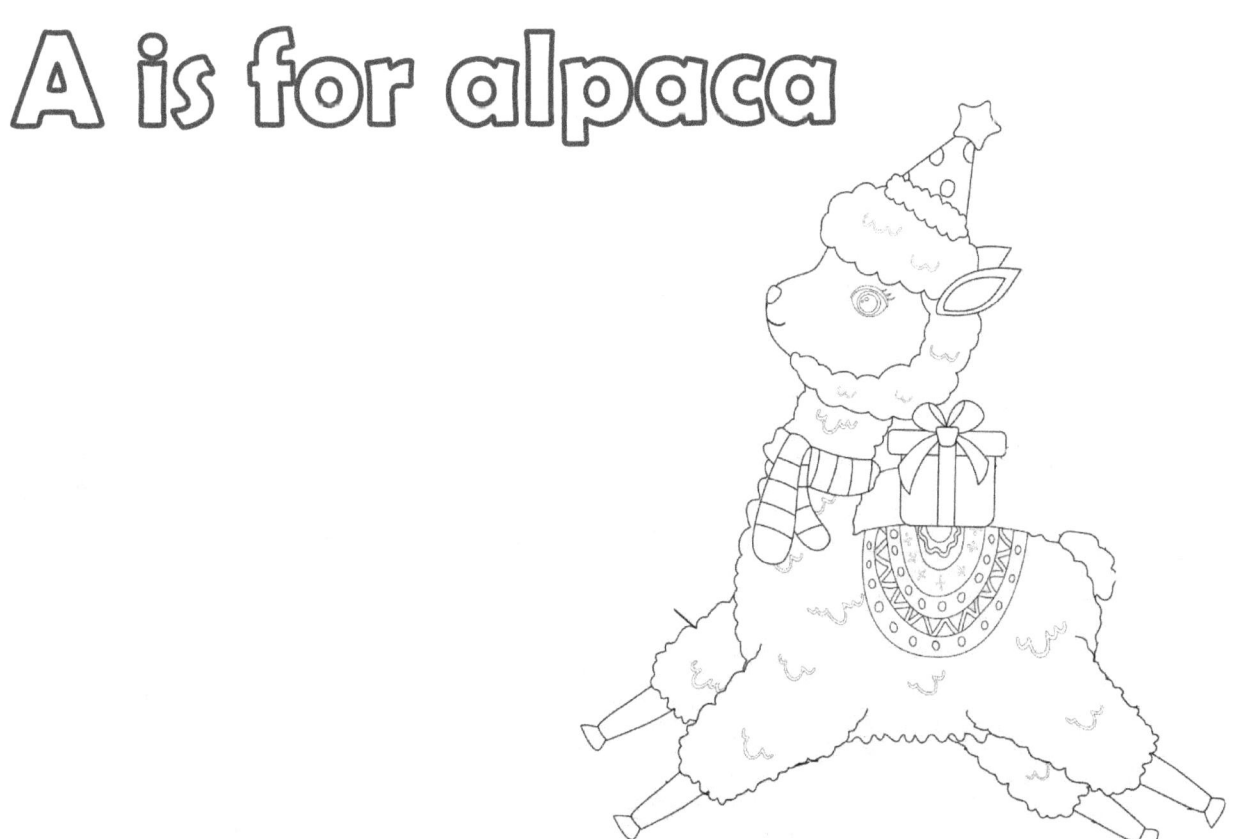

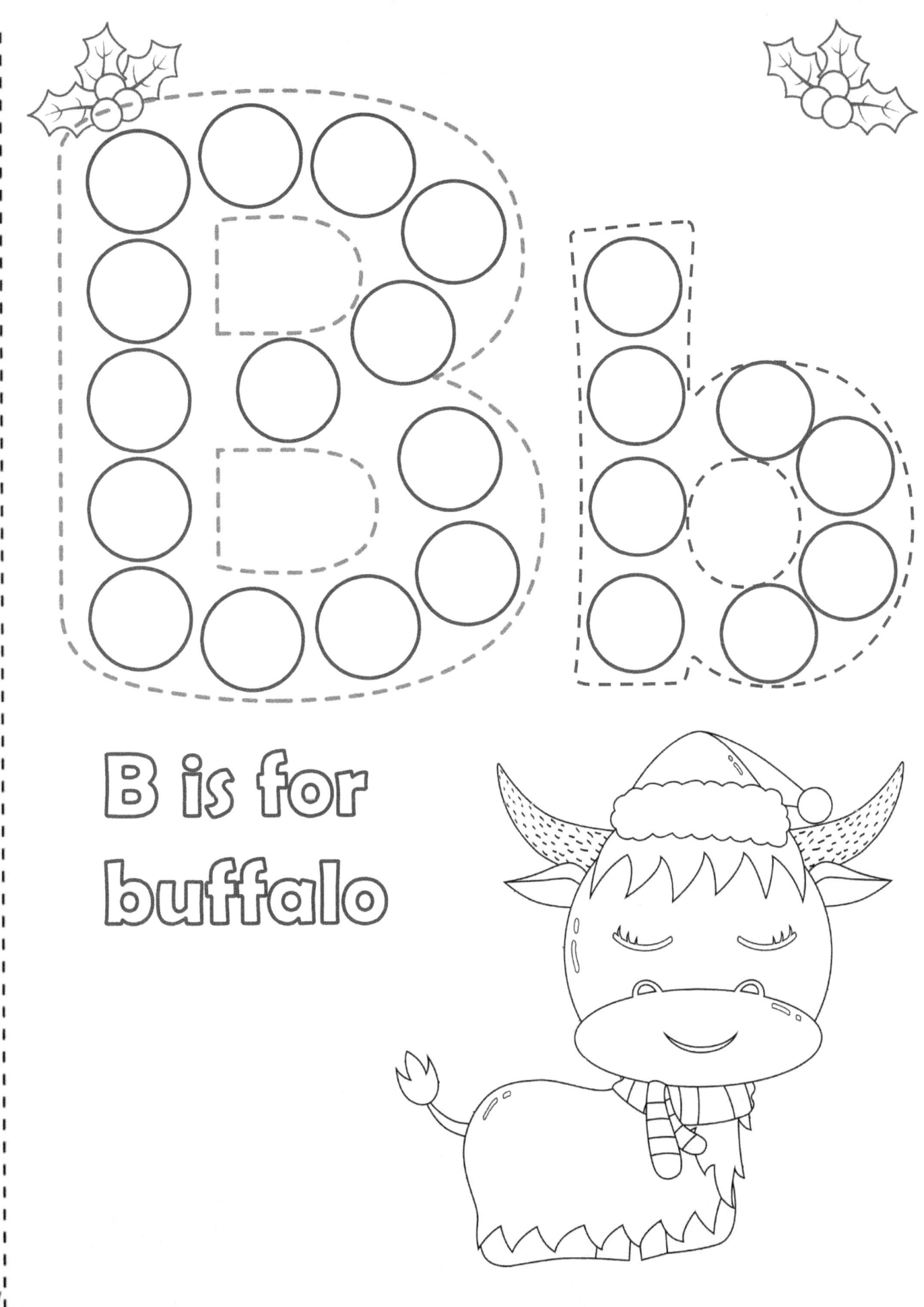

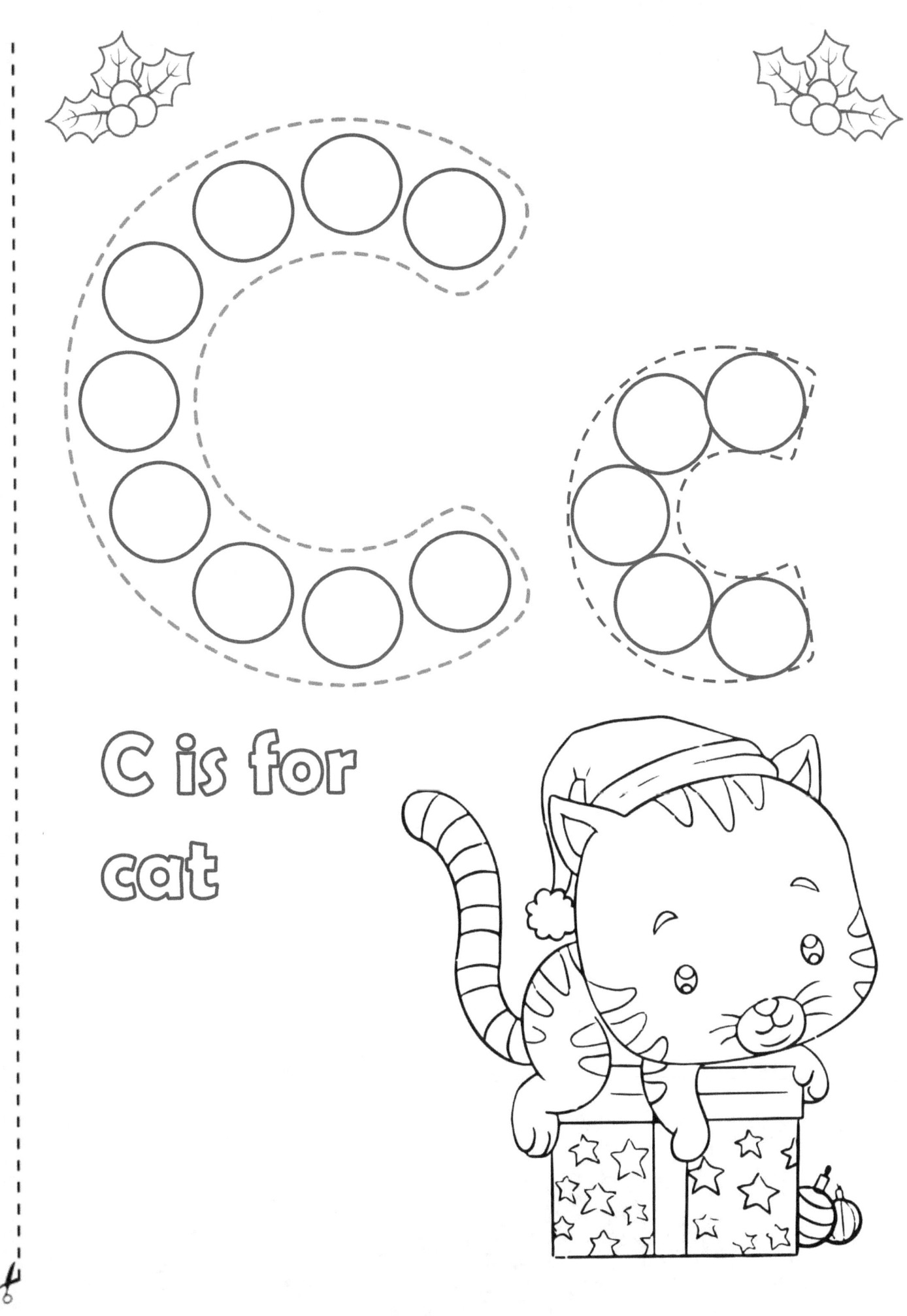

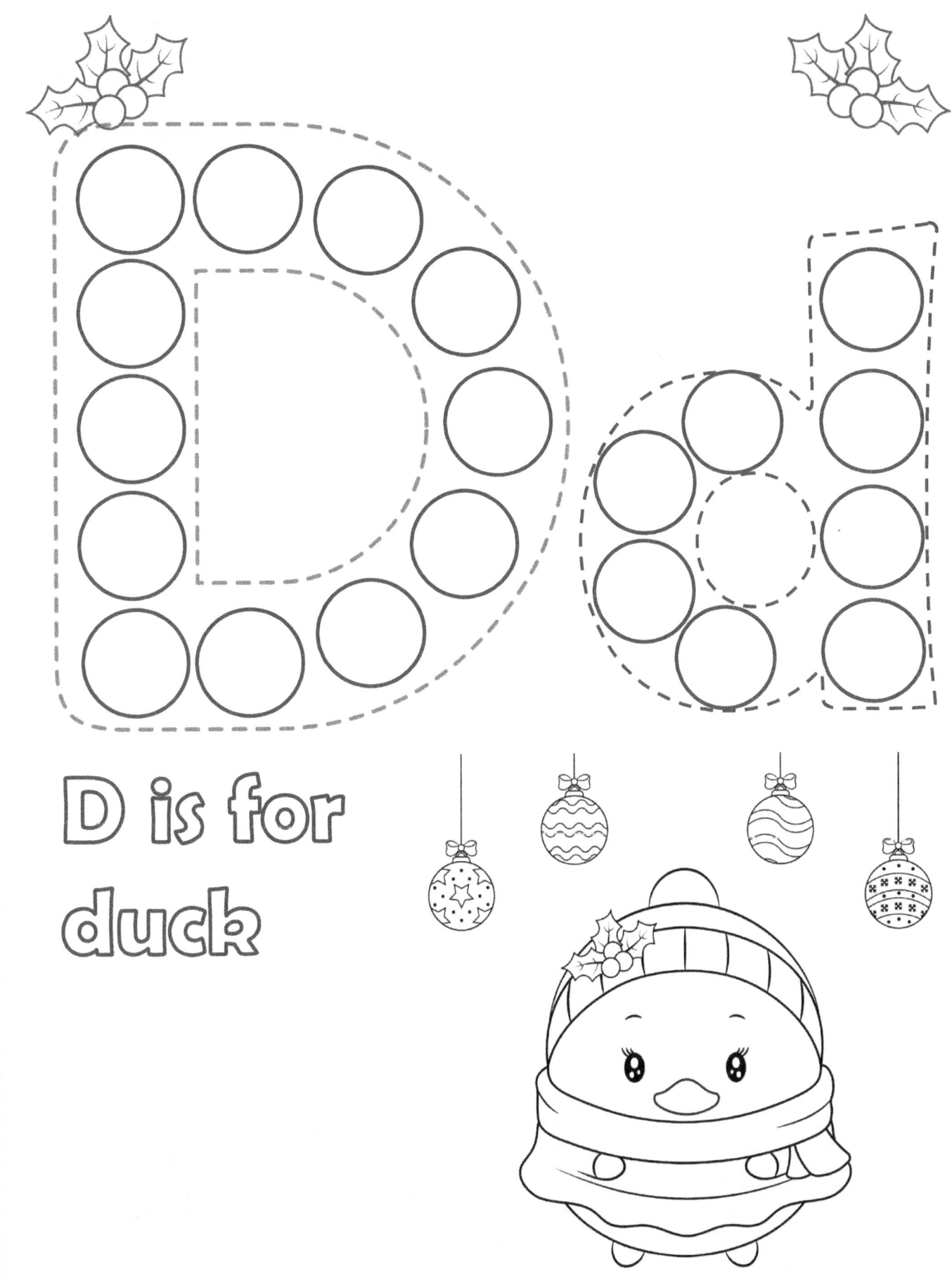

D is for duck

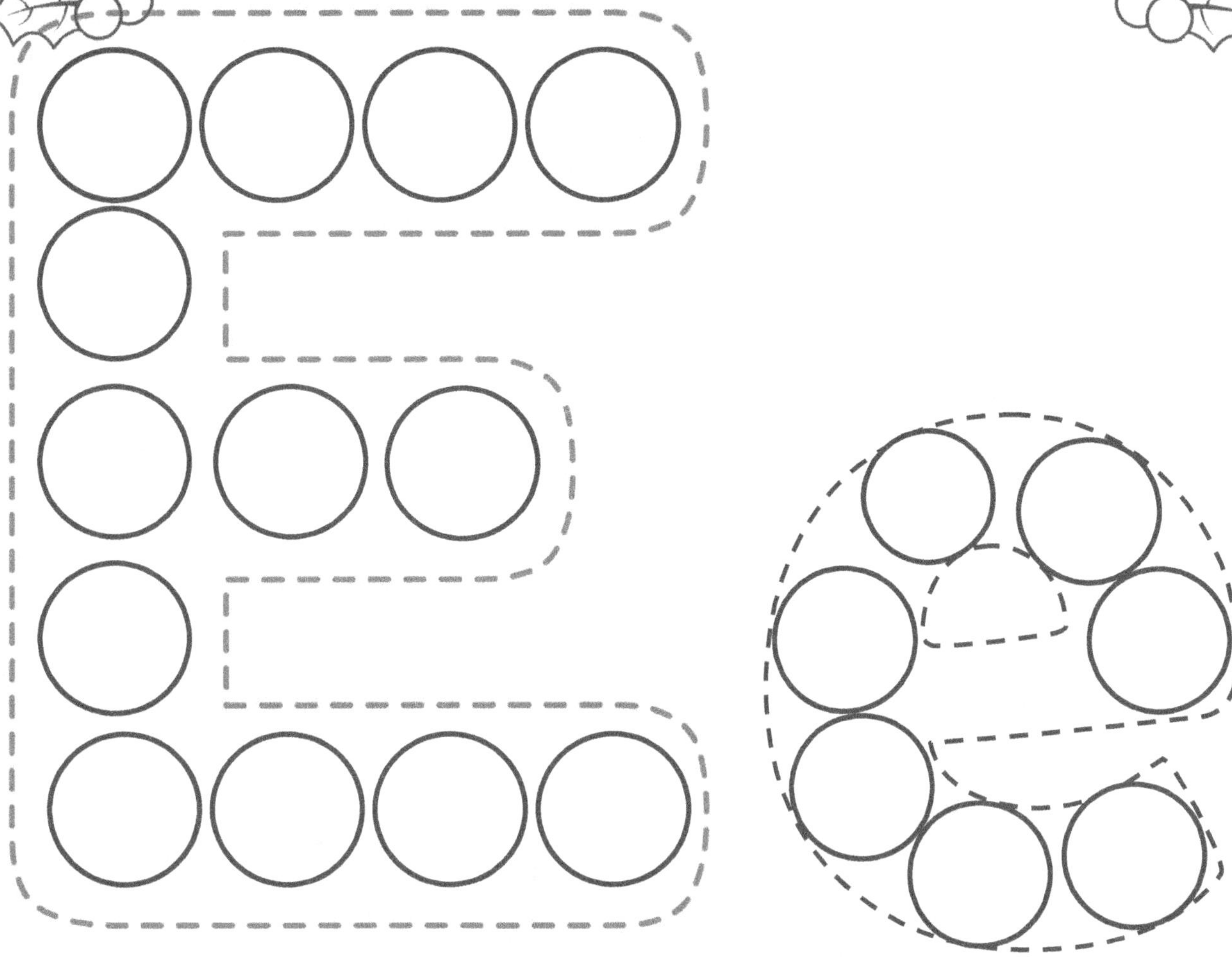

E is for
elephant

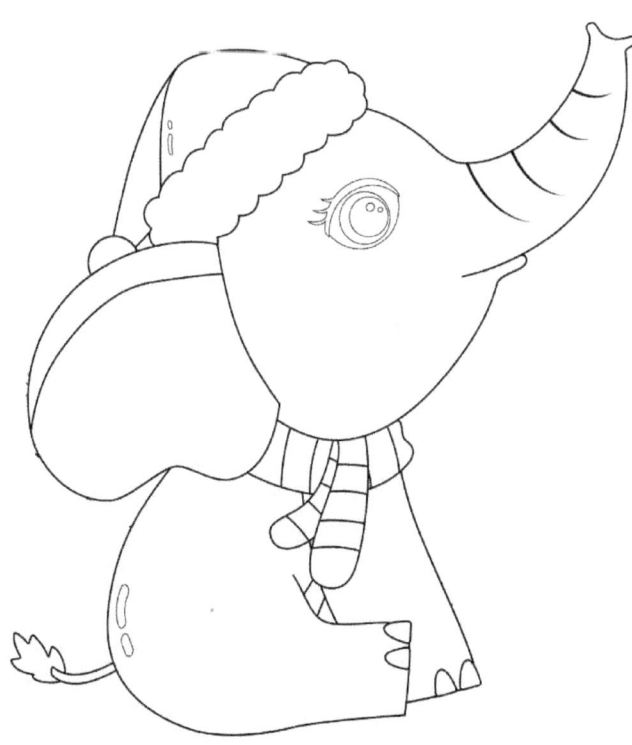

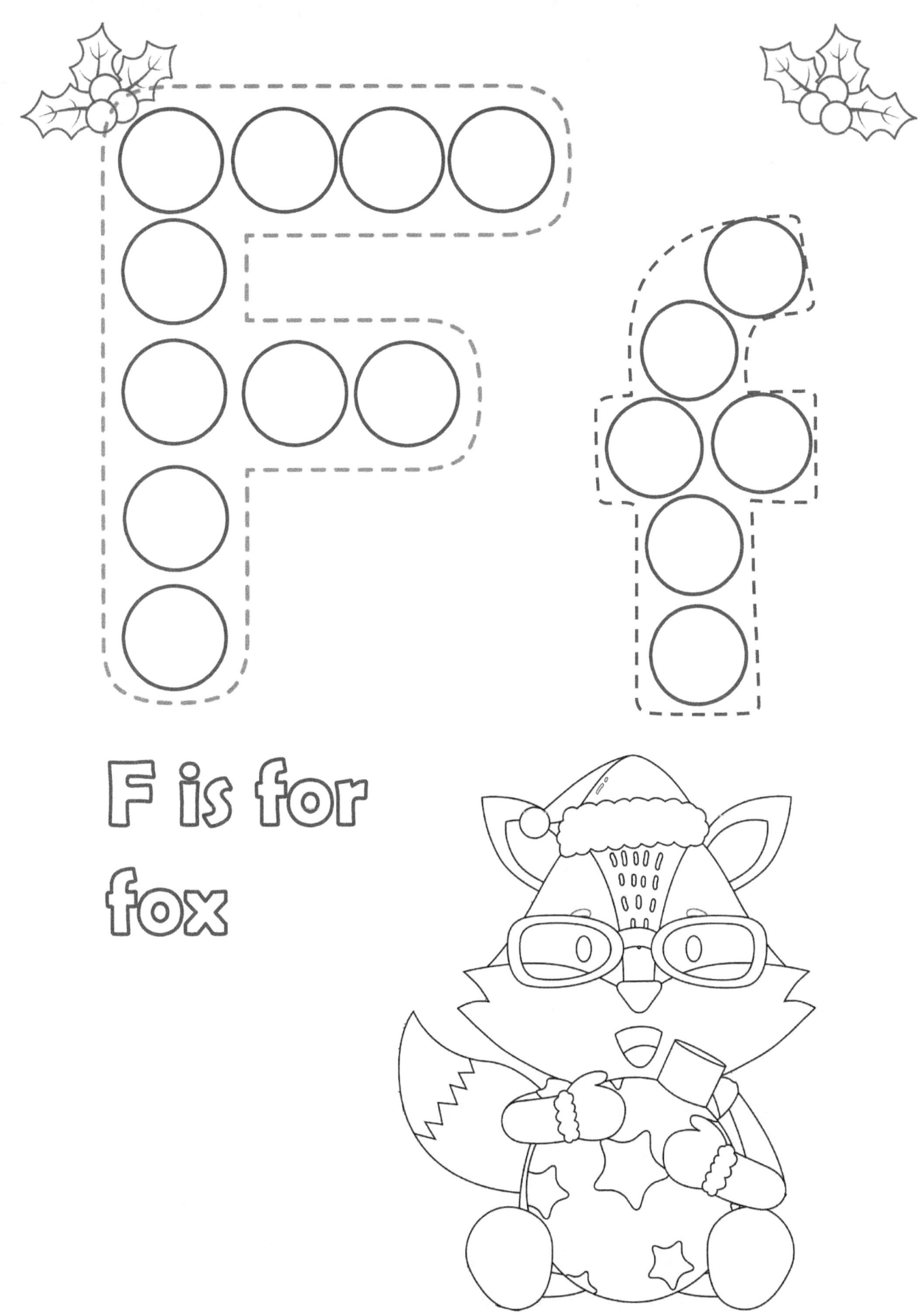

F is for fox

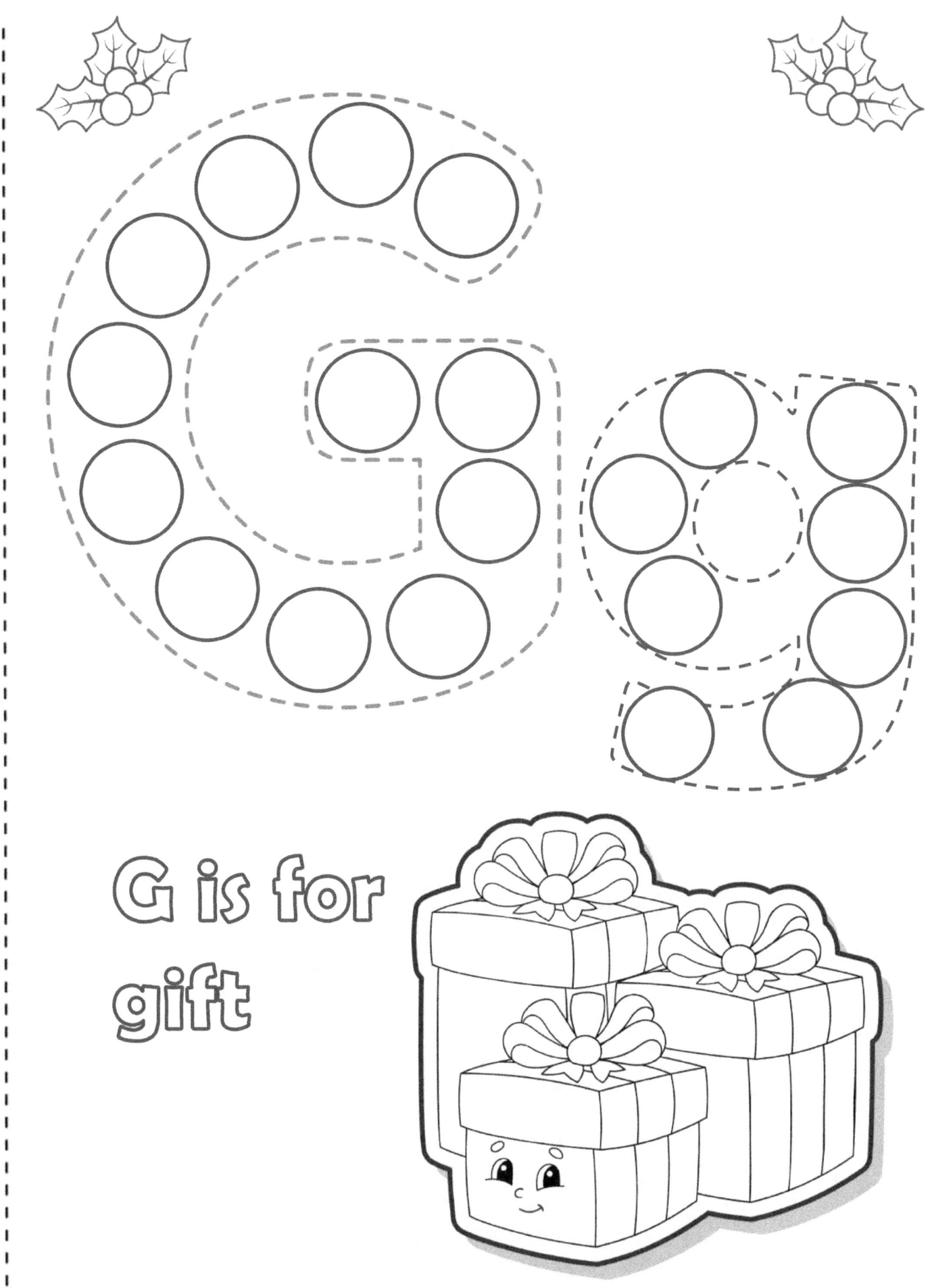

G is for gift

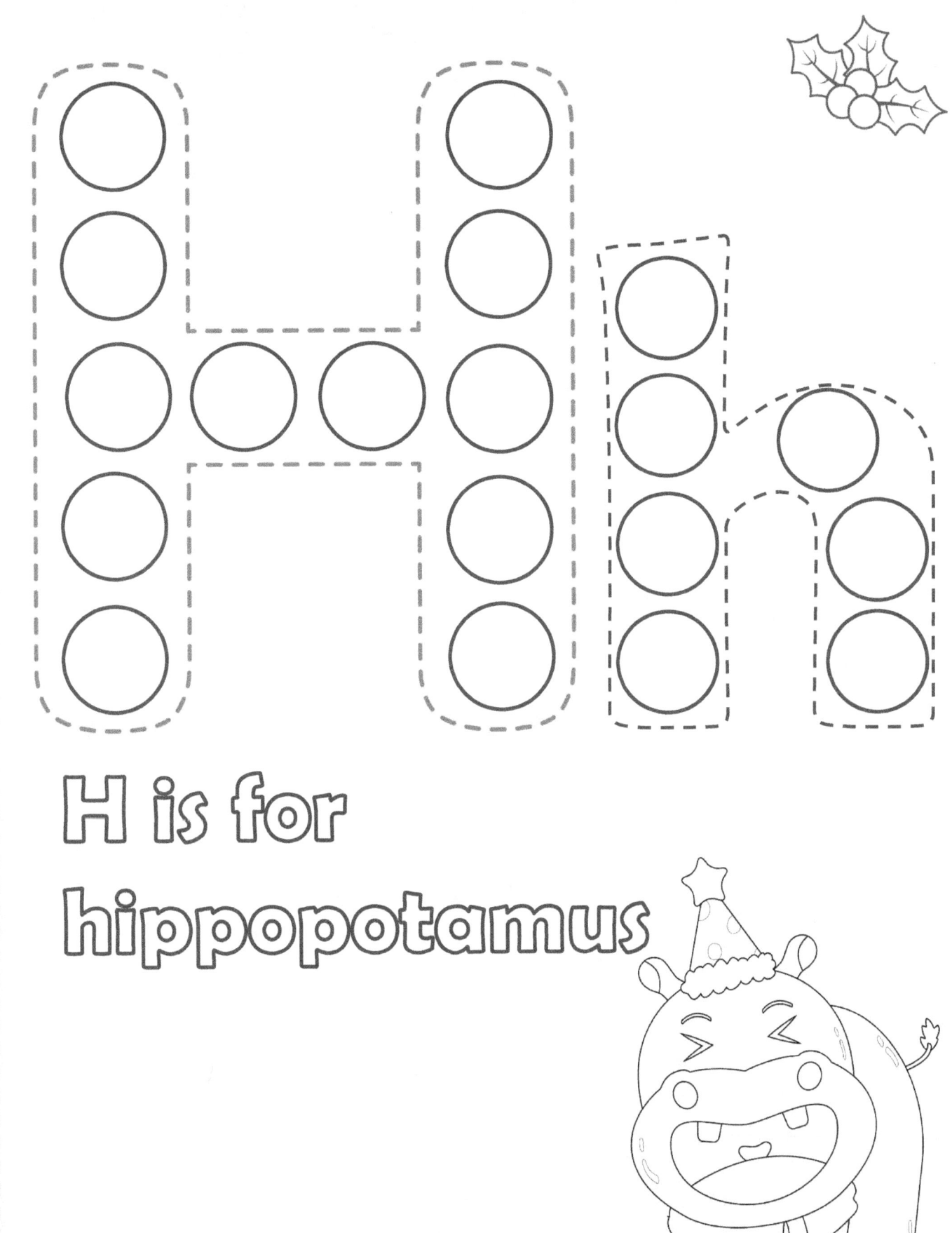

H is for hippopotamus

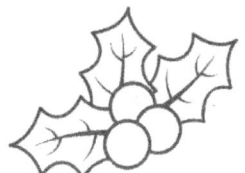
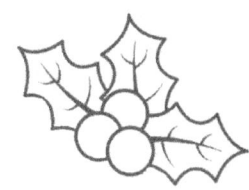
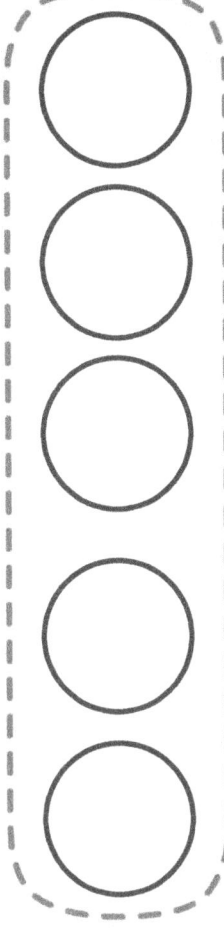
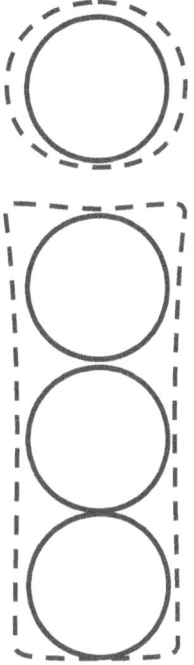

I is for ice skating

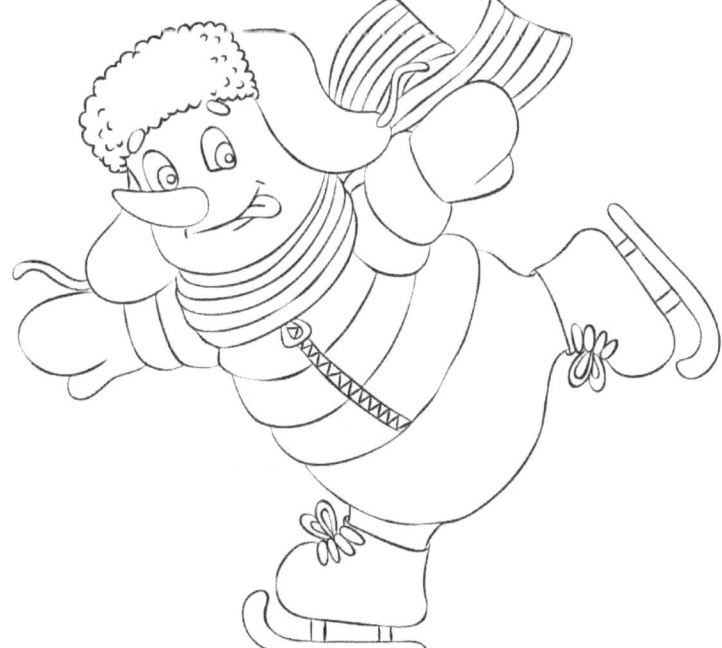

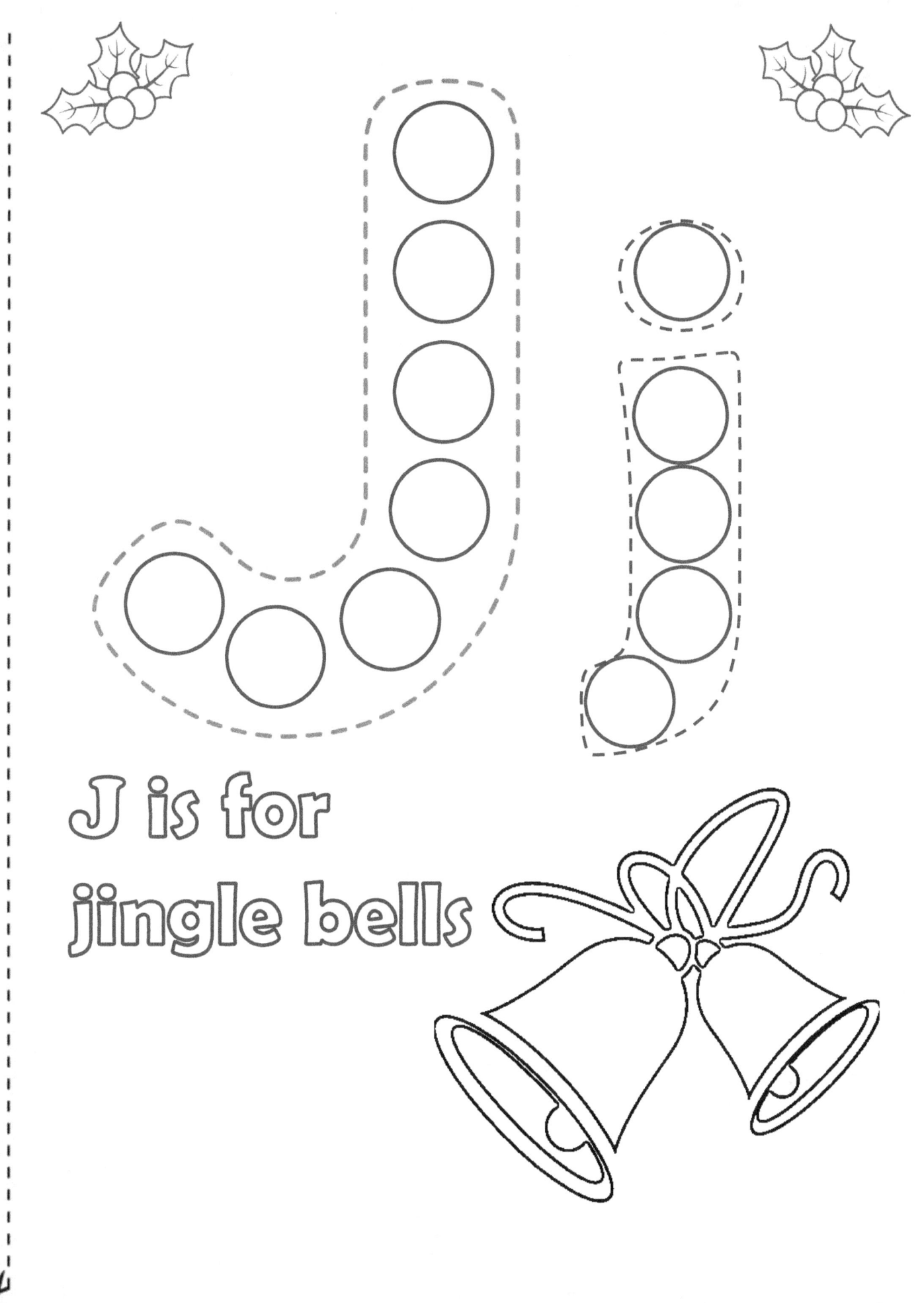

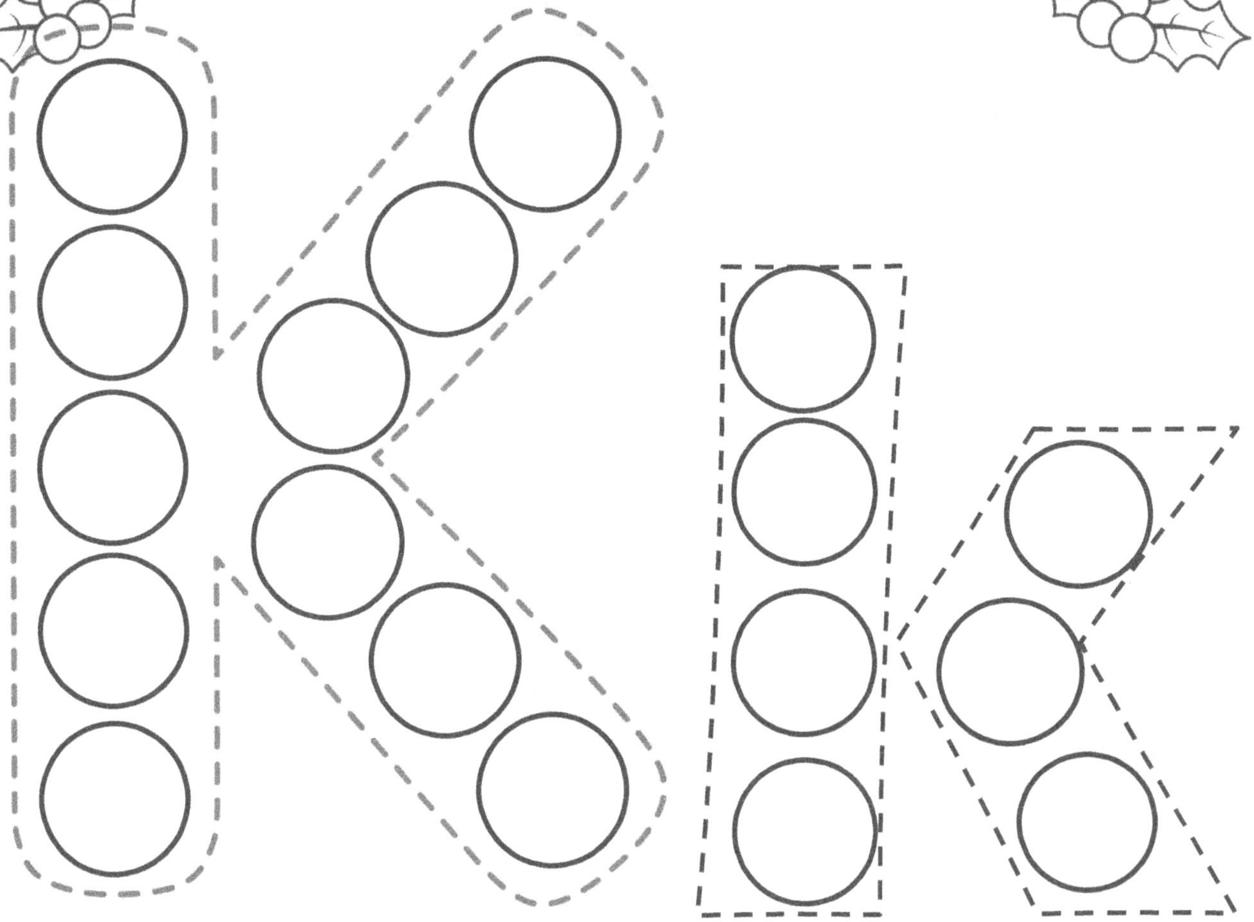

K is for Koala

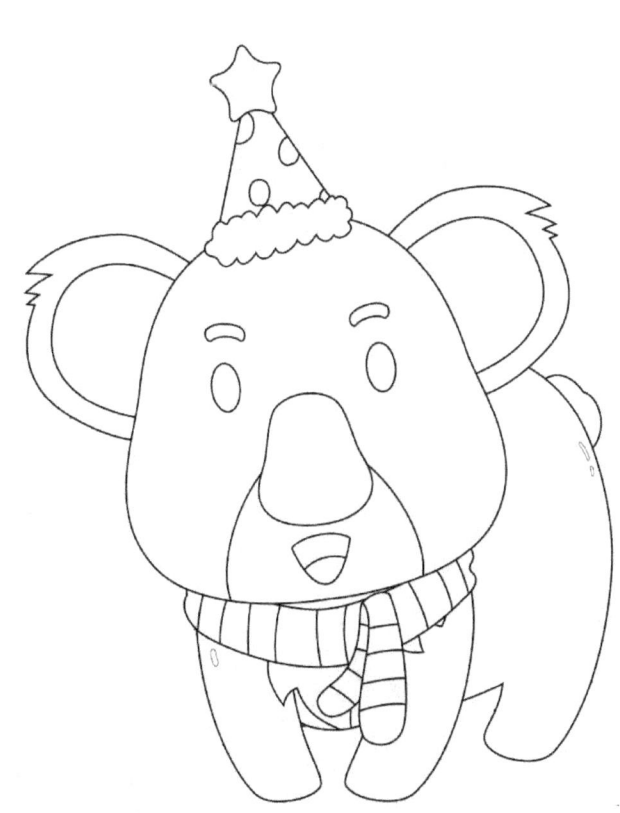

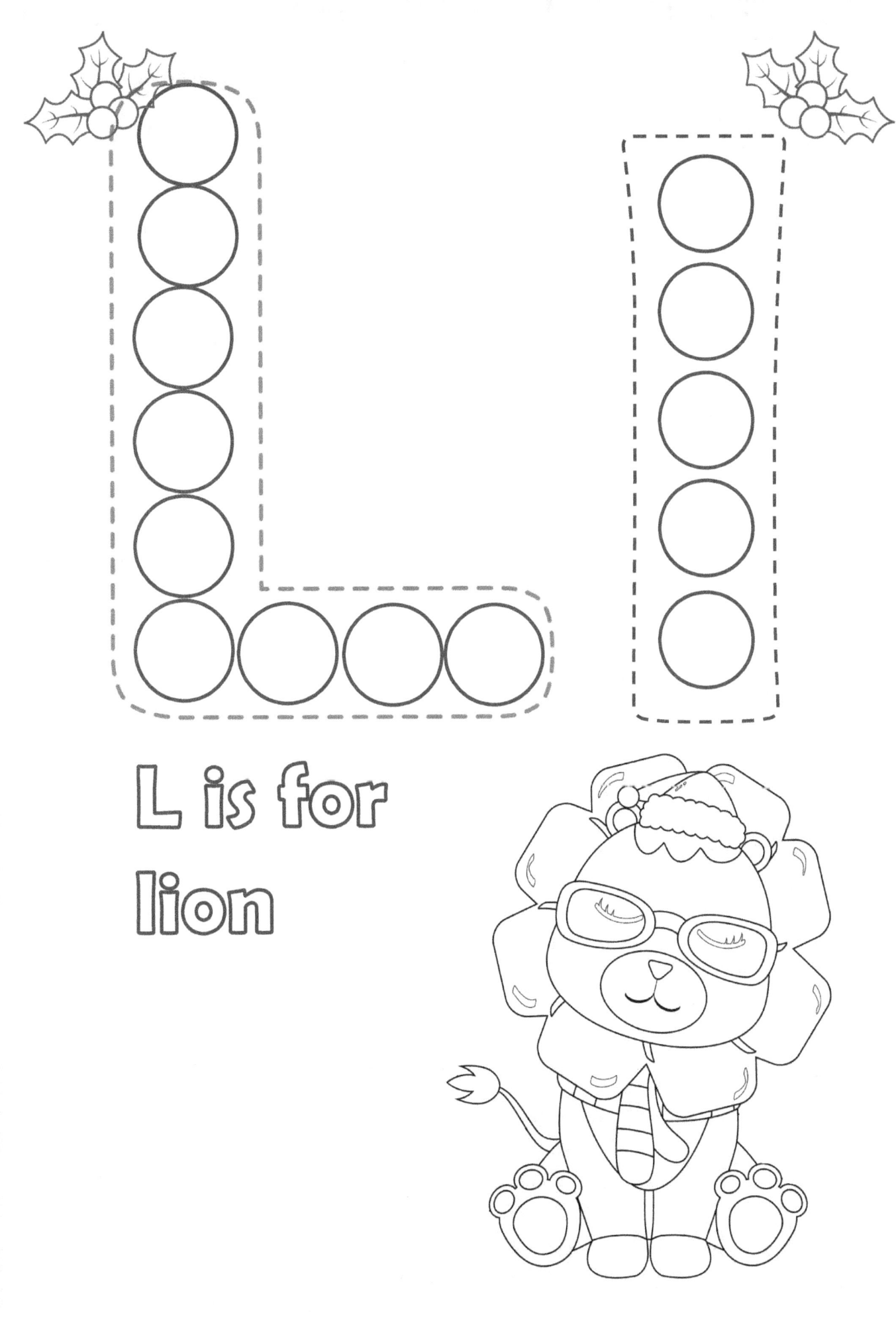

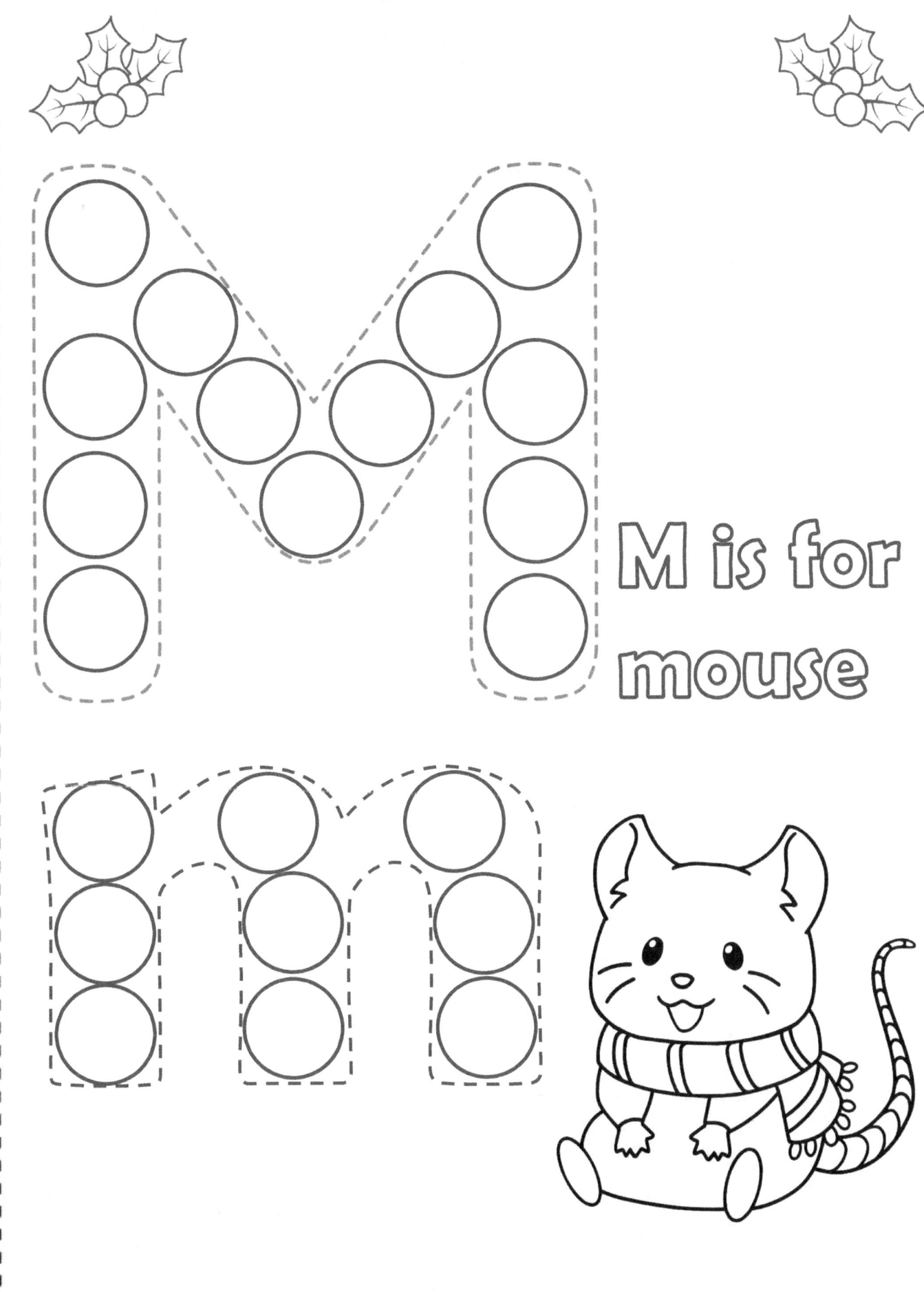

M is for mouse

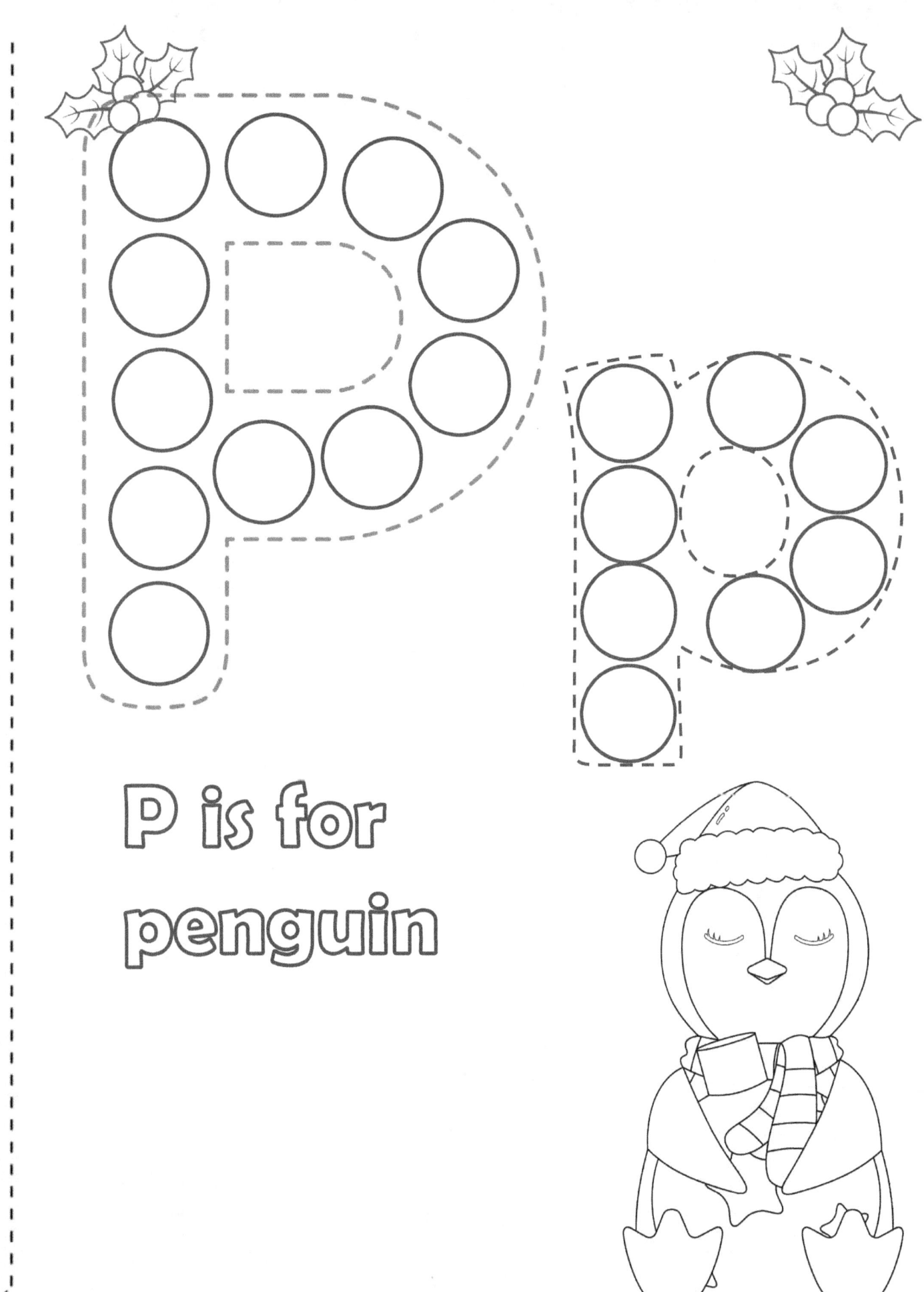

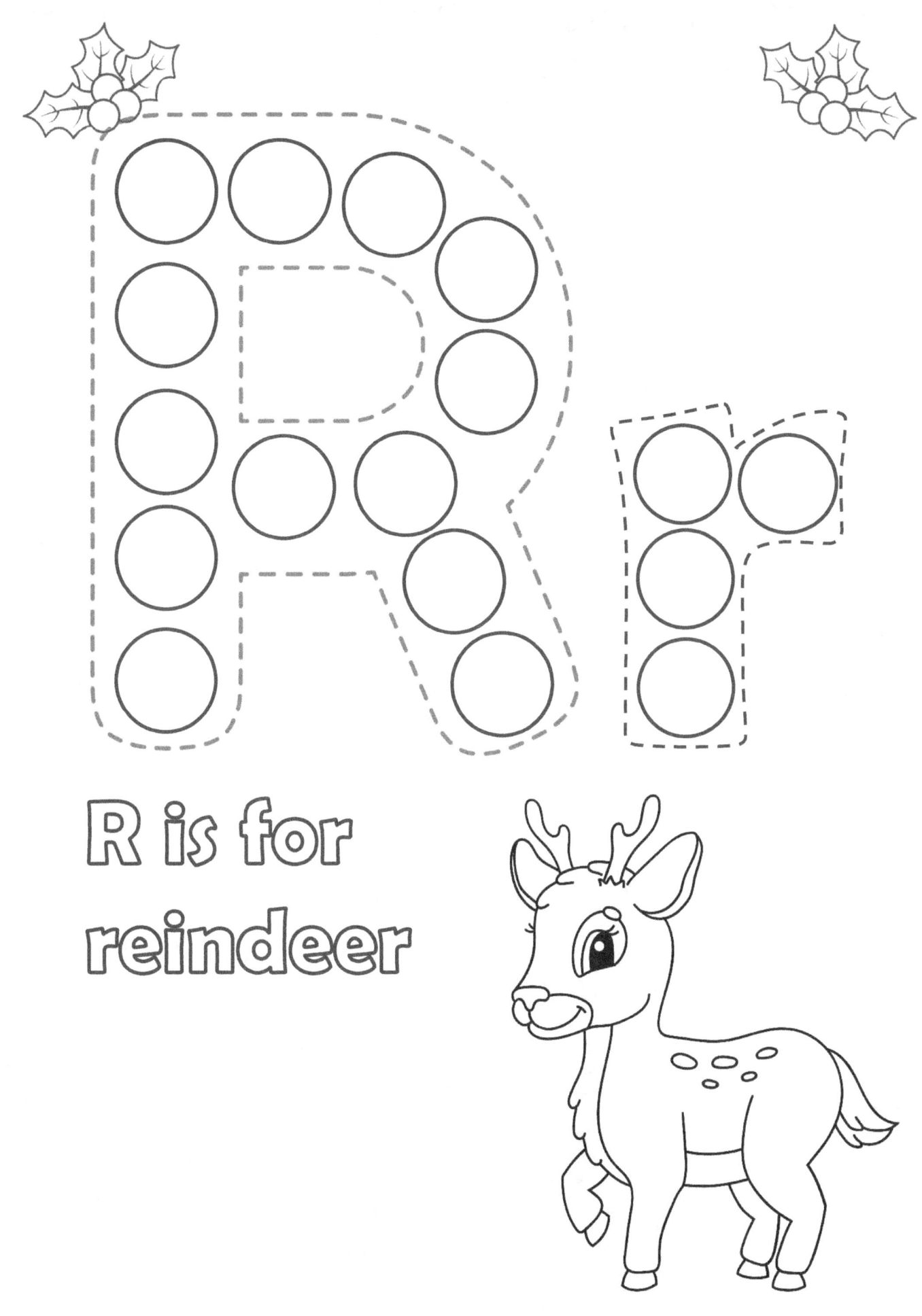

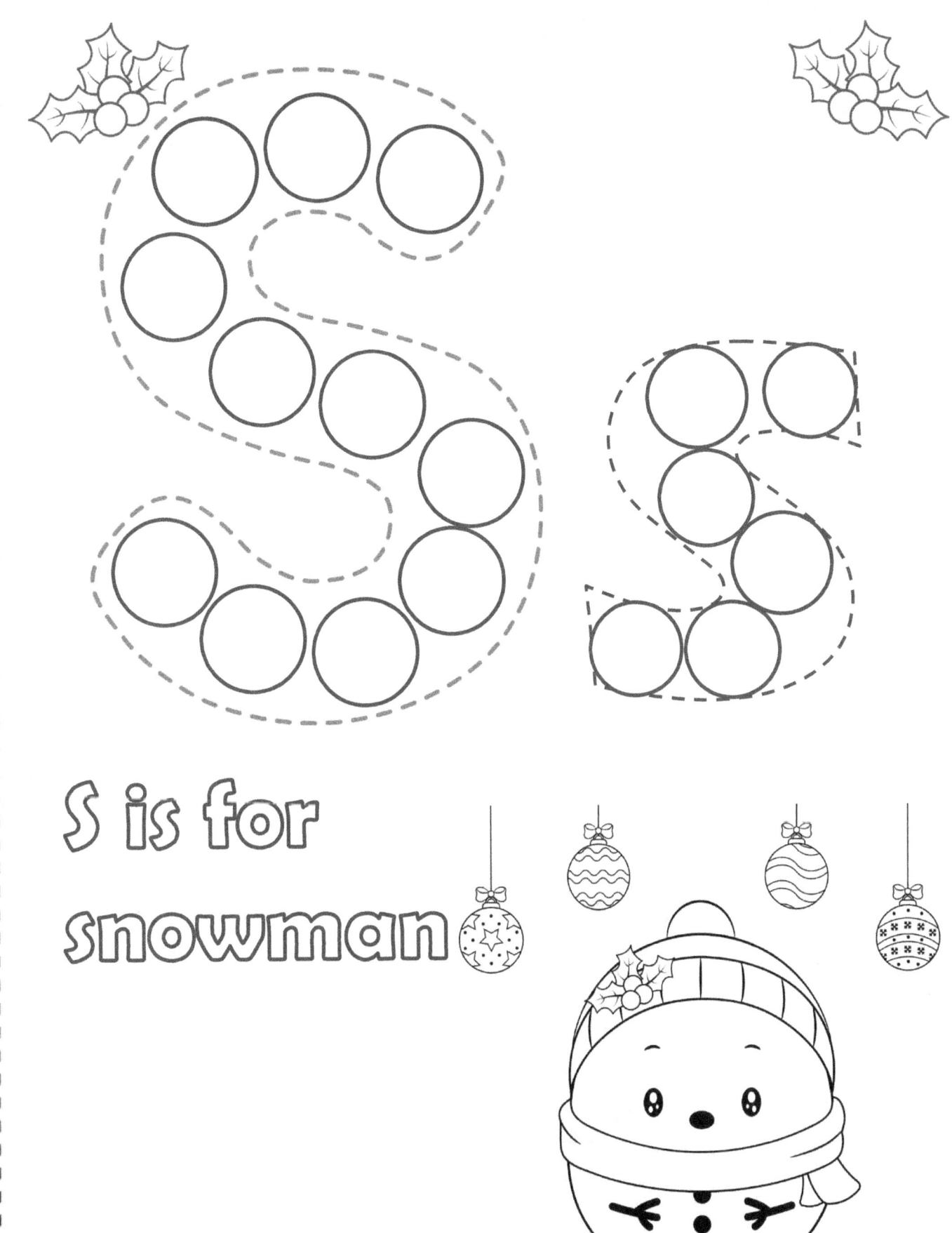

S is for snowman

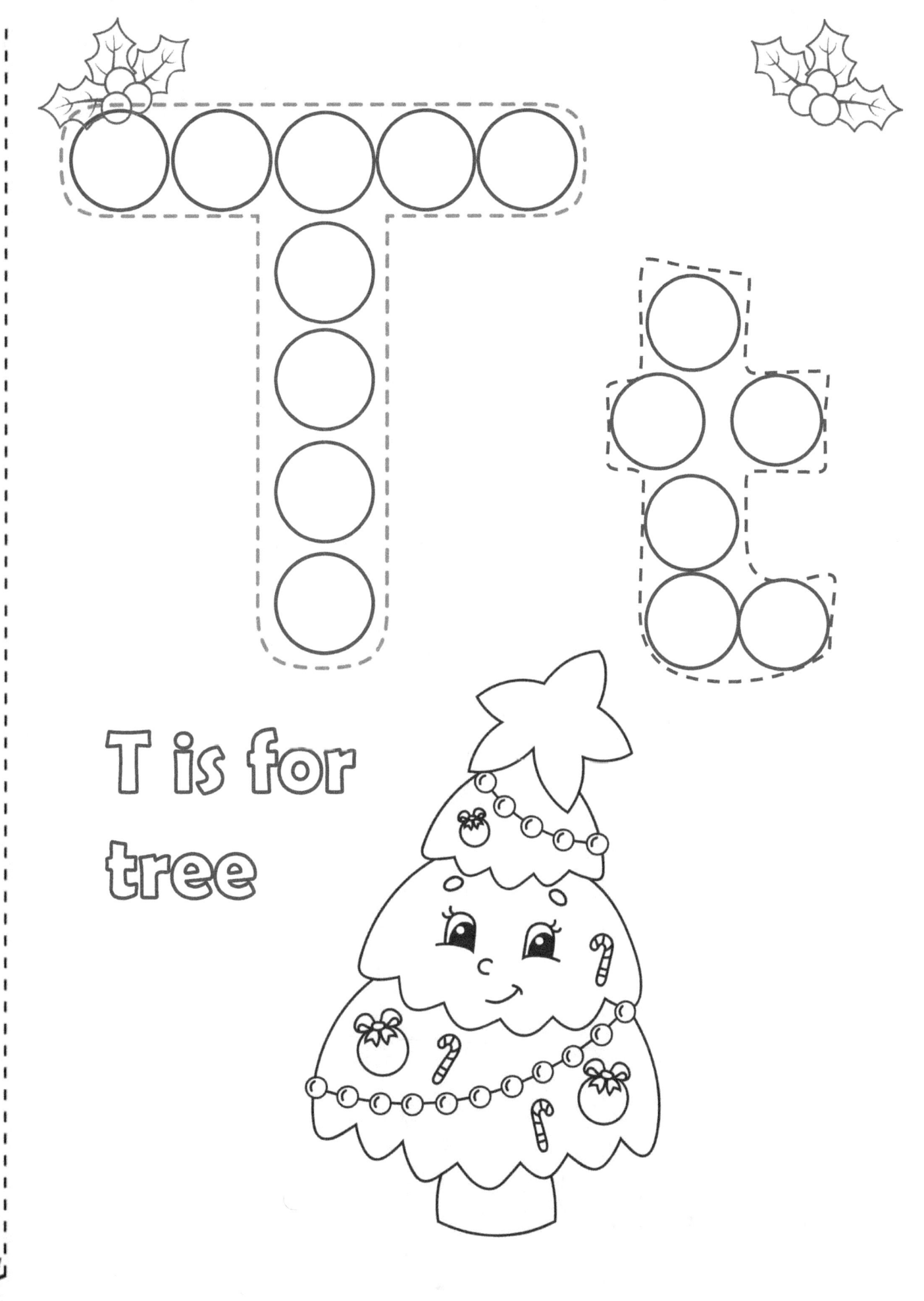

T is for tree

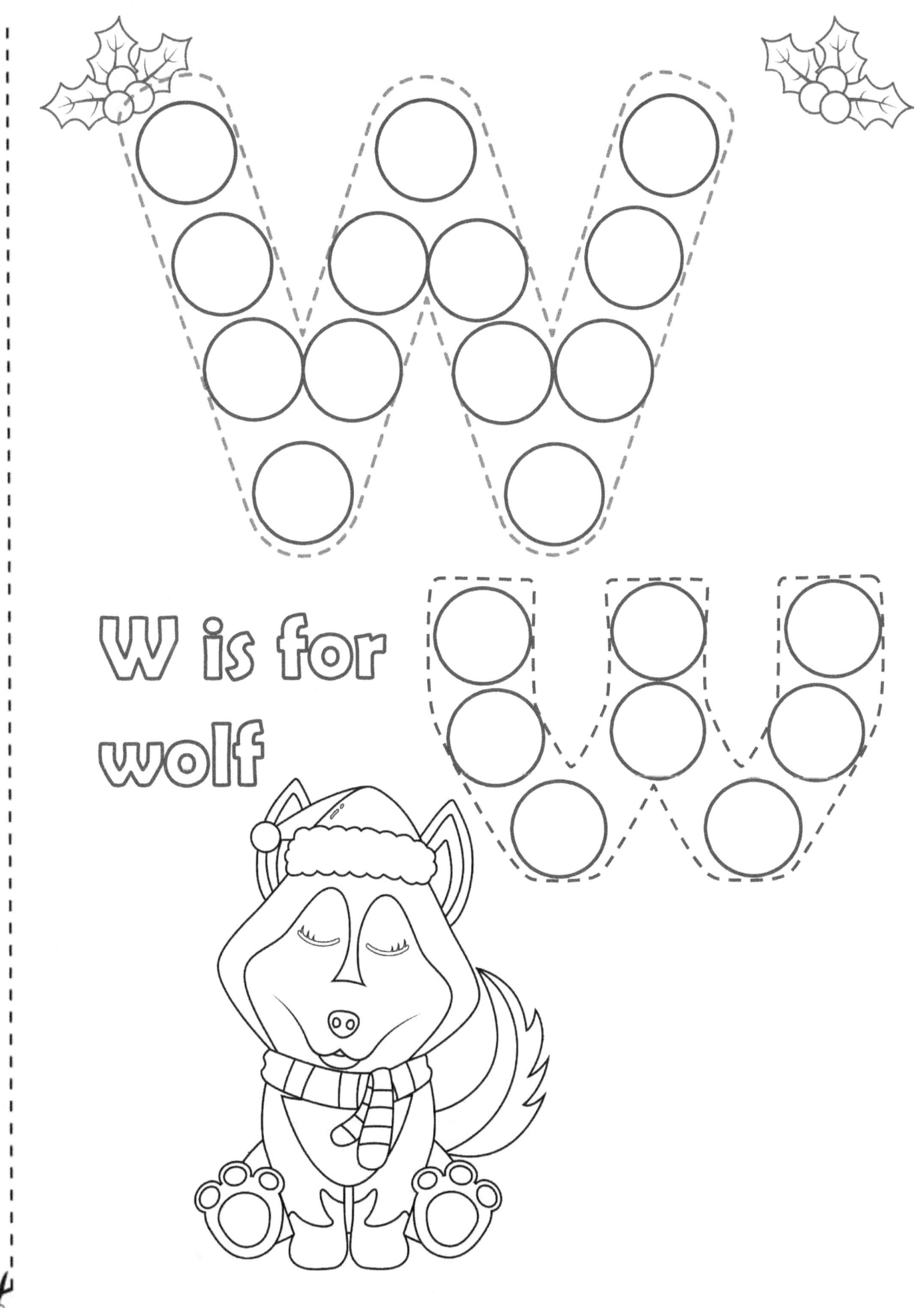

Color all uppercase and lowercase letters Cc is for cat

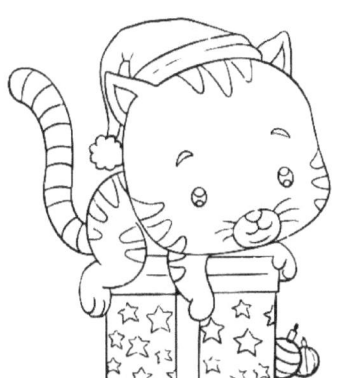

C a p C
 N C c Z
   K   J
  W   c
 c   Q
  C   E
 t   D C

Color all uppercase and lowercase letters

Ee is for elephant

E Z h O
   f   e
L m N q
   N M G
I J
E V e O
   Q d E

Color all uppercase and lowercase letters

Mm is for mouse

m e M j

a k W m

t f t k

M n M

e h n

m A j k

Color all uppercase and lowercase letters

Rr is for reindeer

p d R M y
r E c n r
k d i y K b
c R a k w s
   r   R   a
v   d P p

Find, color, and write the missing letters

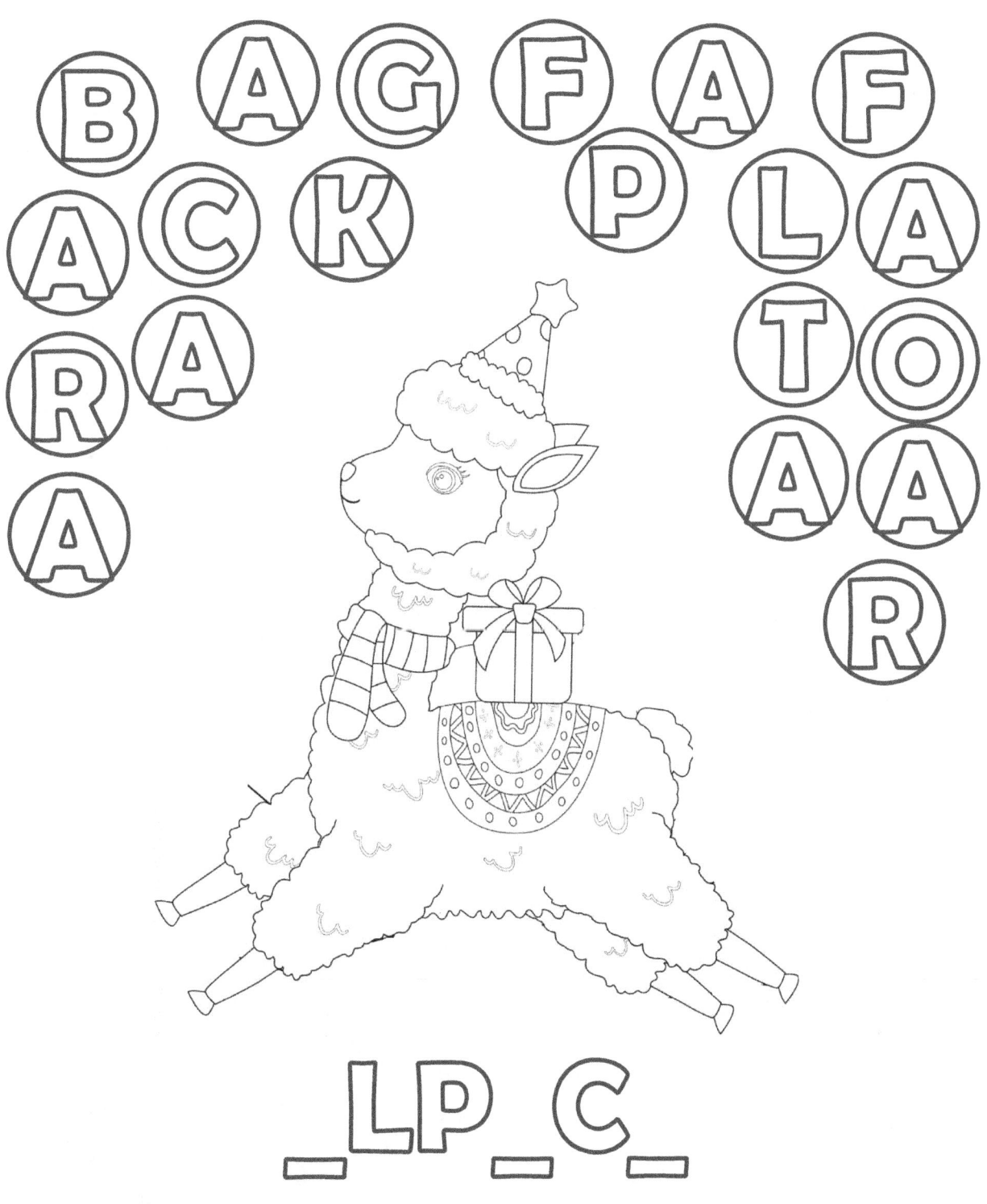

_ L P _ C _

Find, color, and write the missing letters

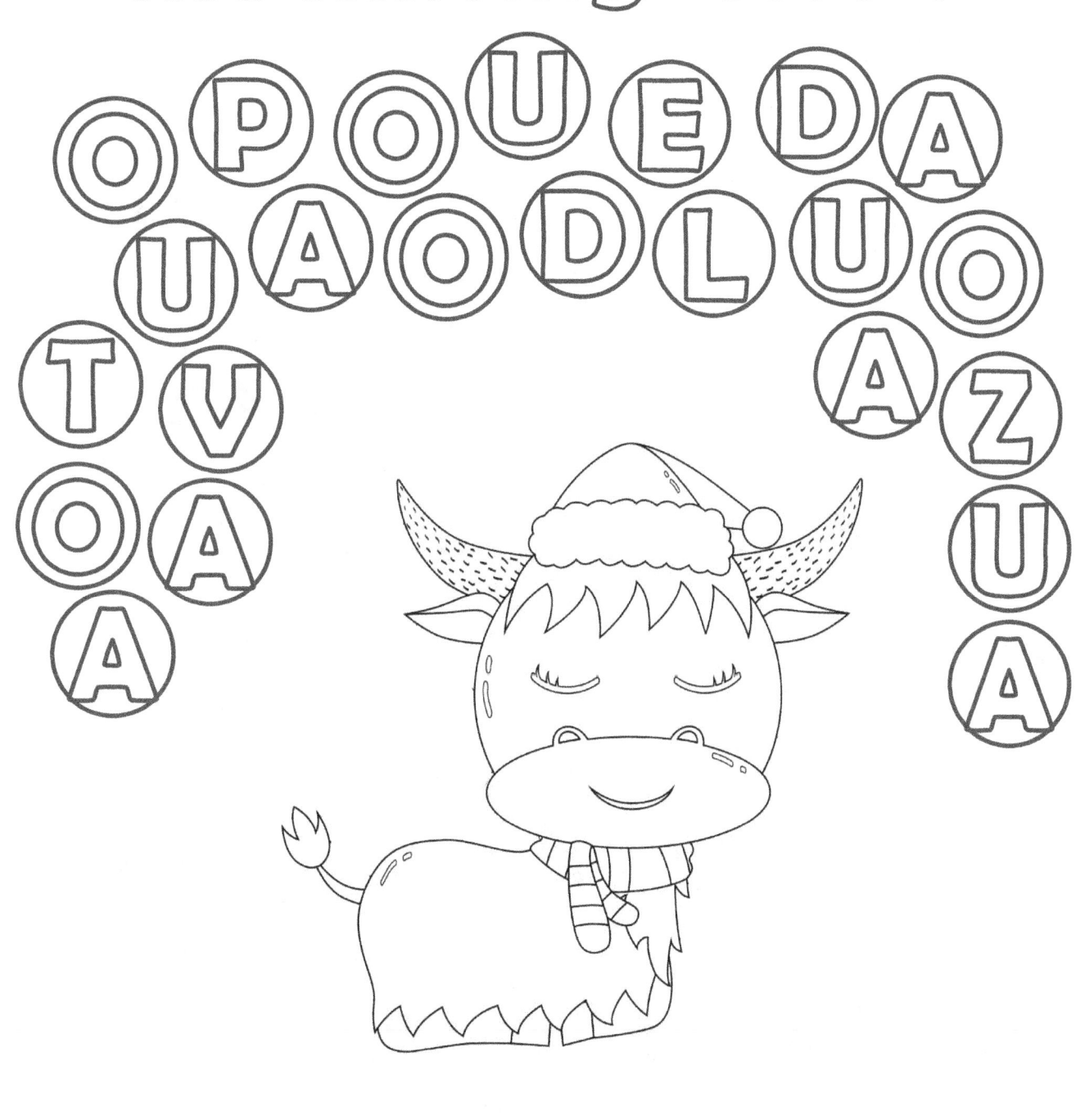

B_FF_L_

Find, color, and write the missing letters

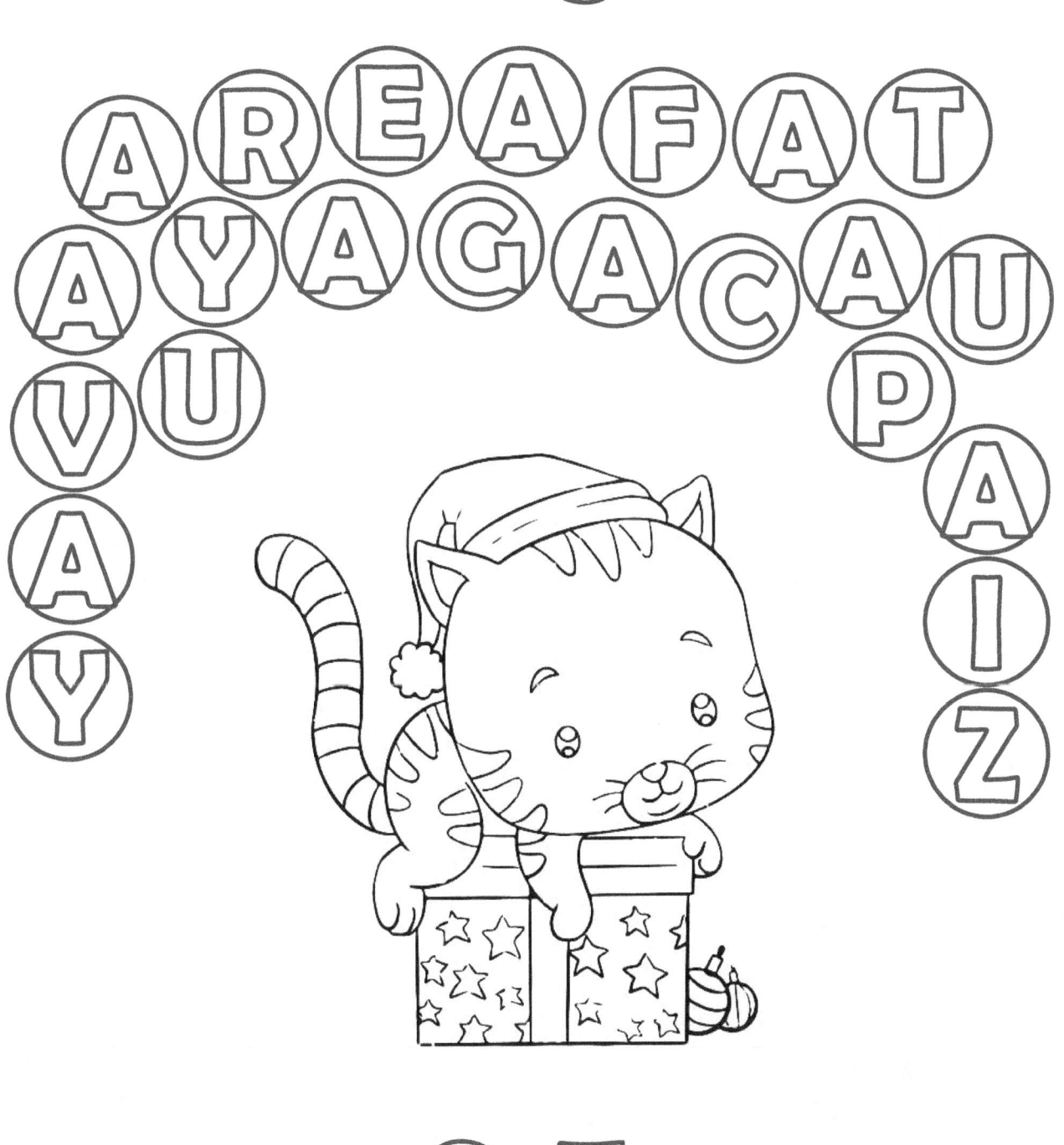

C_T

Find, color, and write the missing letters

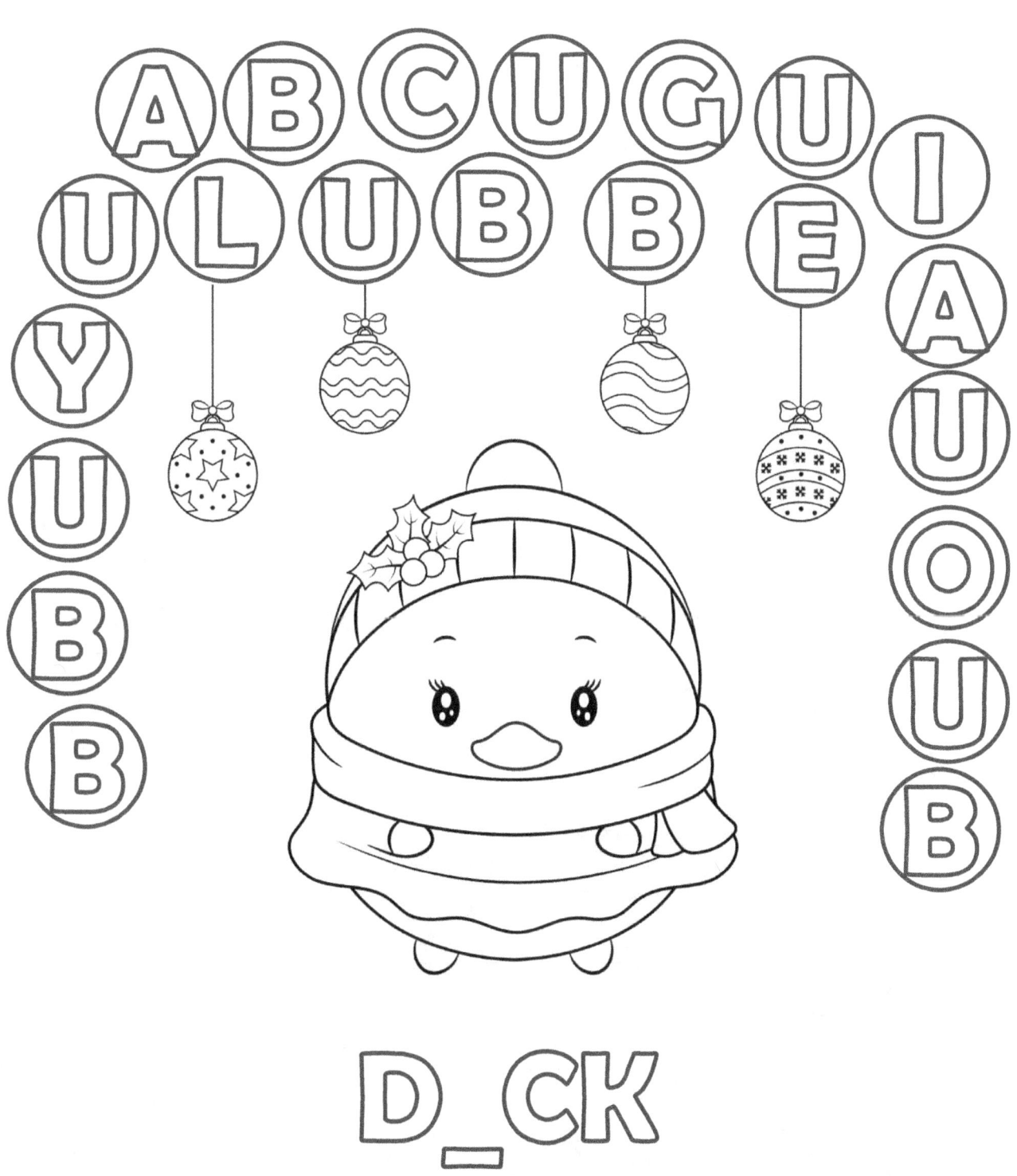

D_CK

Find, color, and write the missing letters

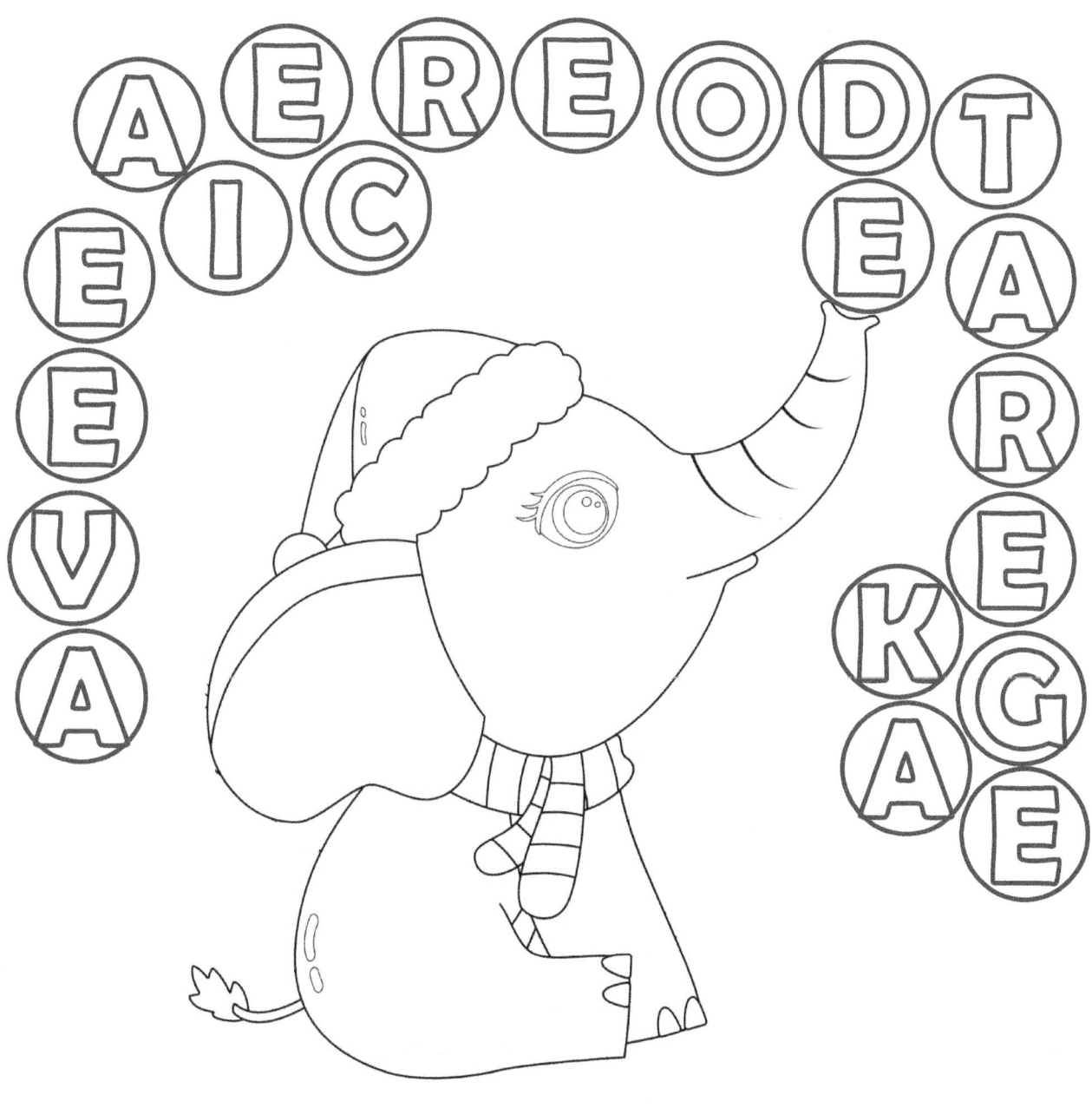

_ L _ P H _ N T

Find, color, and write the missing letters

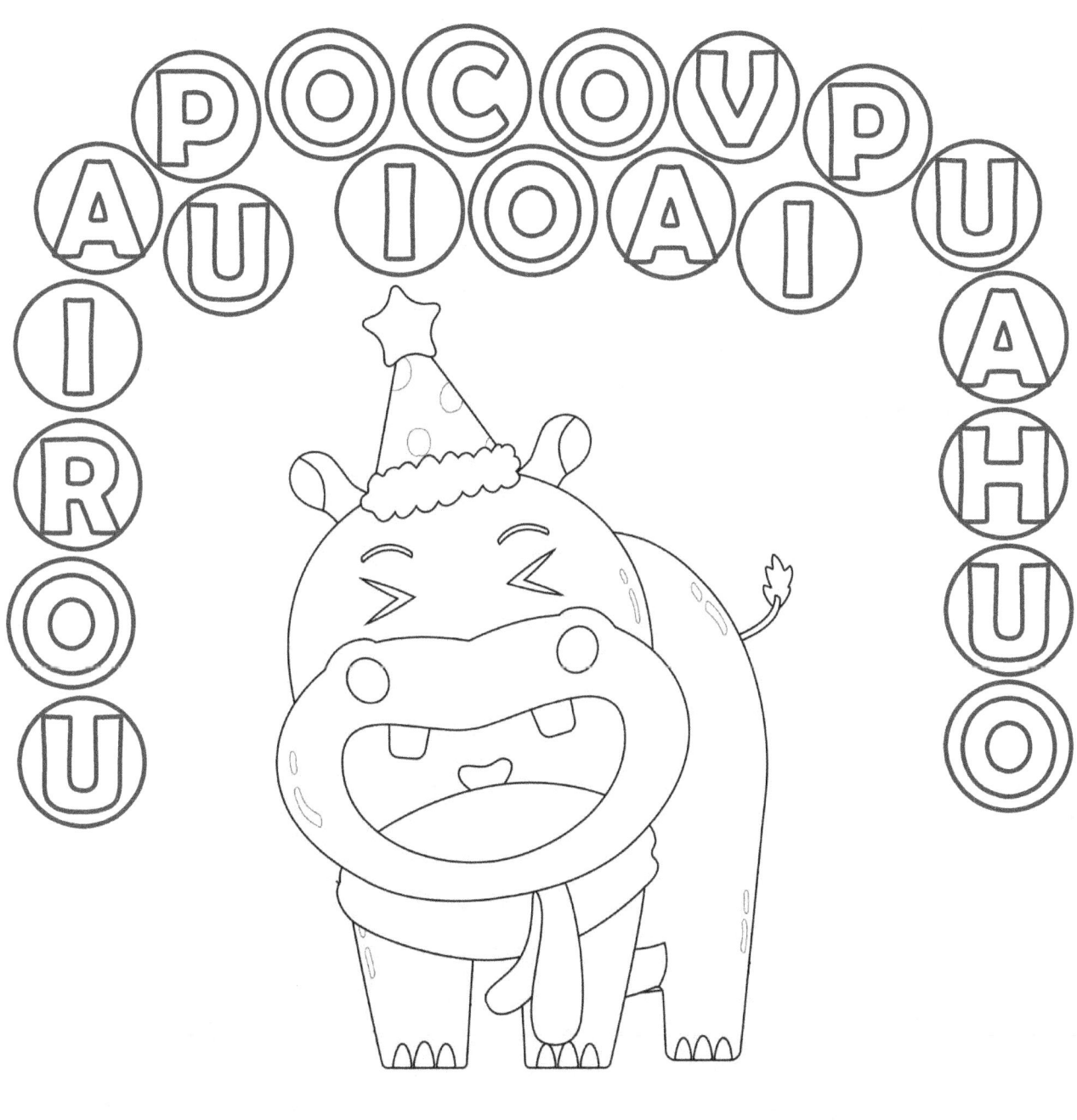

H_PP_P_T_M_S

Find, color, and write the missing letters

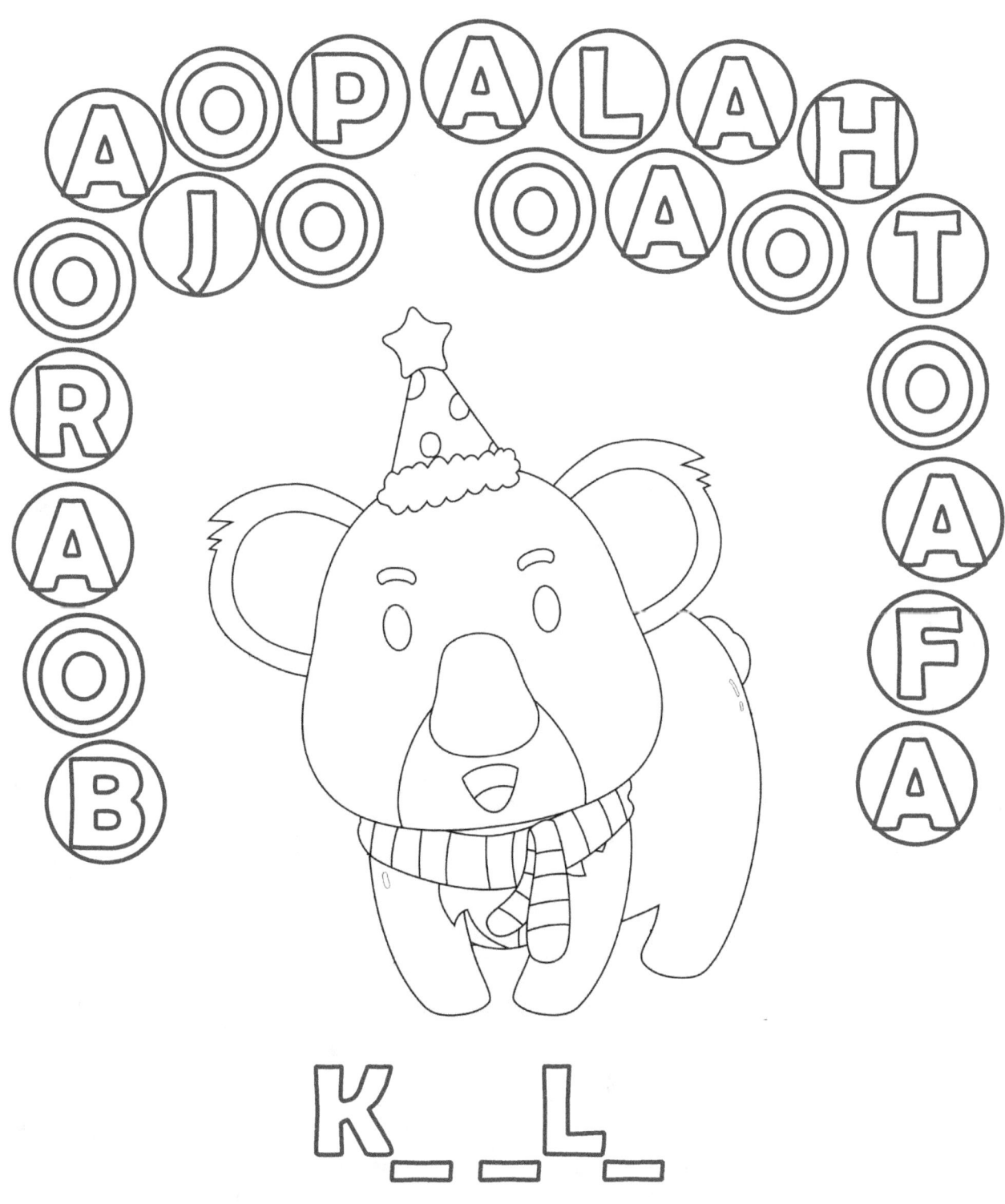

K _ _ L _

Find, color, and write the missing letters

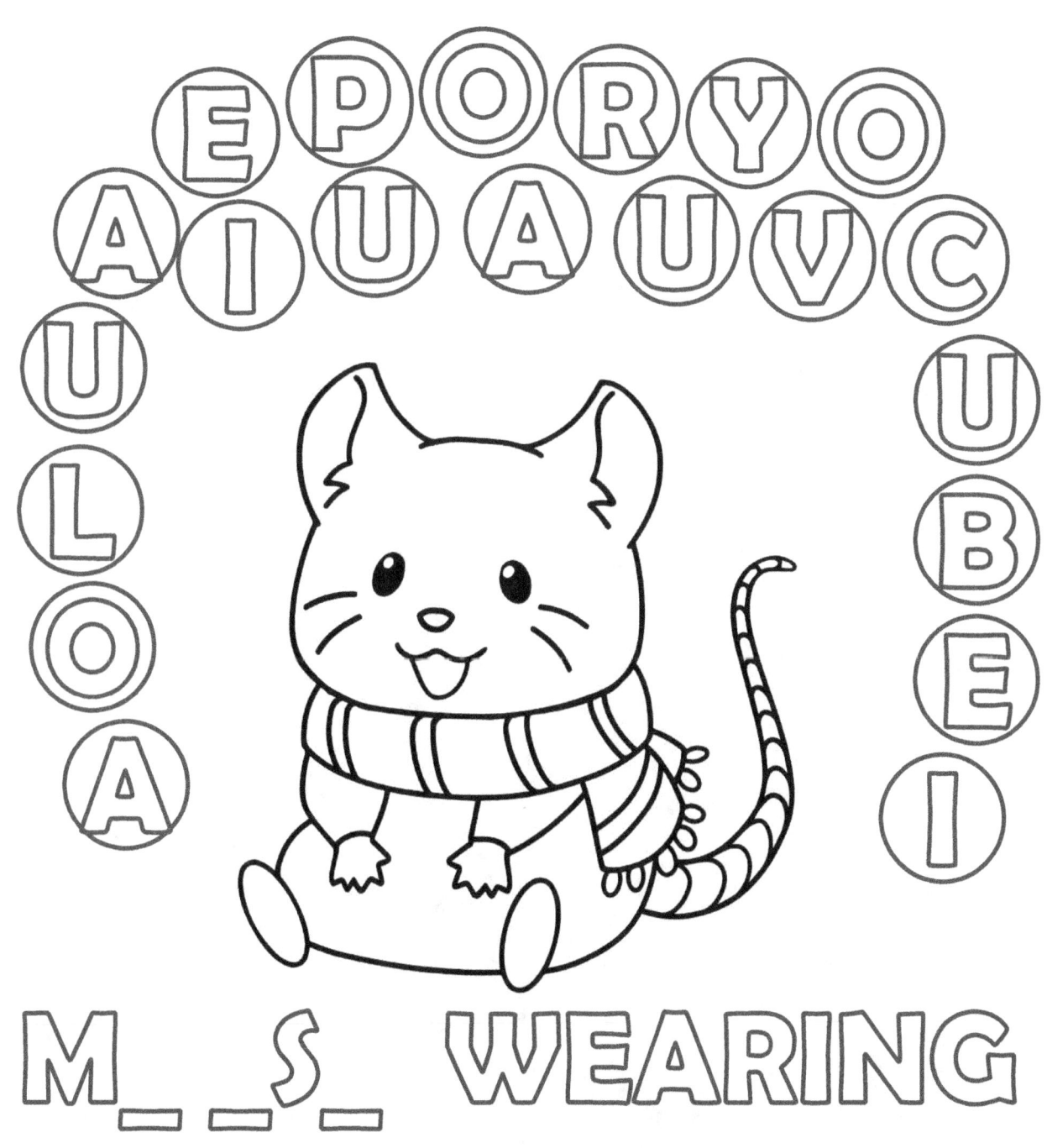

M_ _S_ WEARING A SCARF

Find, color, and write the missing letters

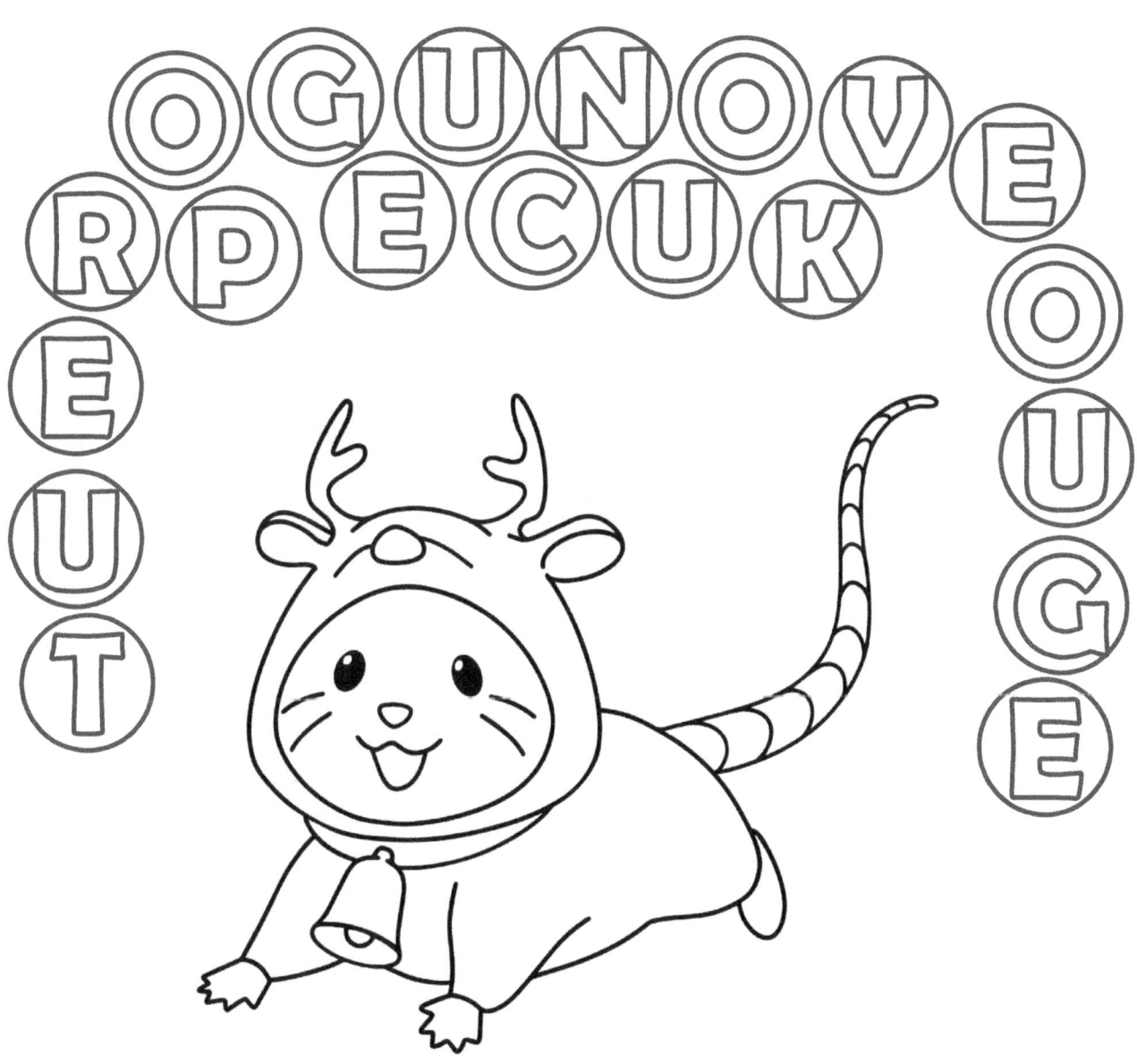

MOUSE WEARING A C_ST_M_

Find, color, and write the missing letters

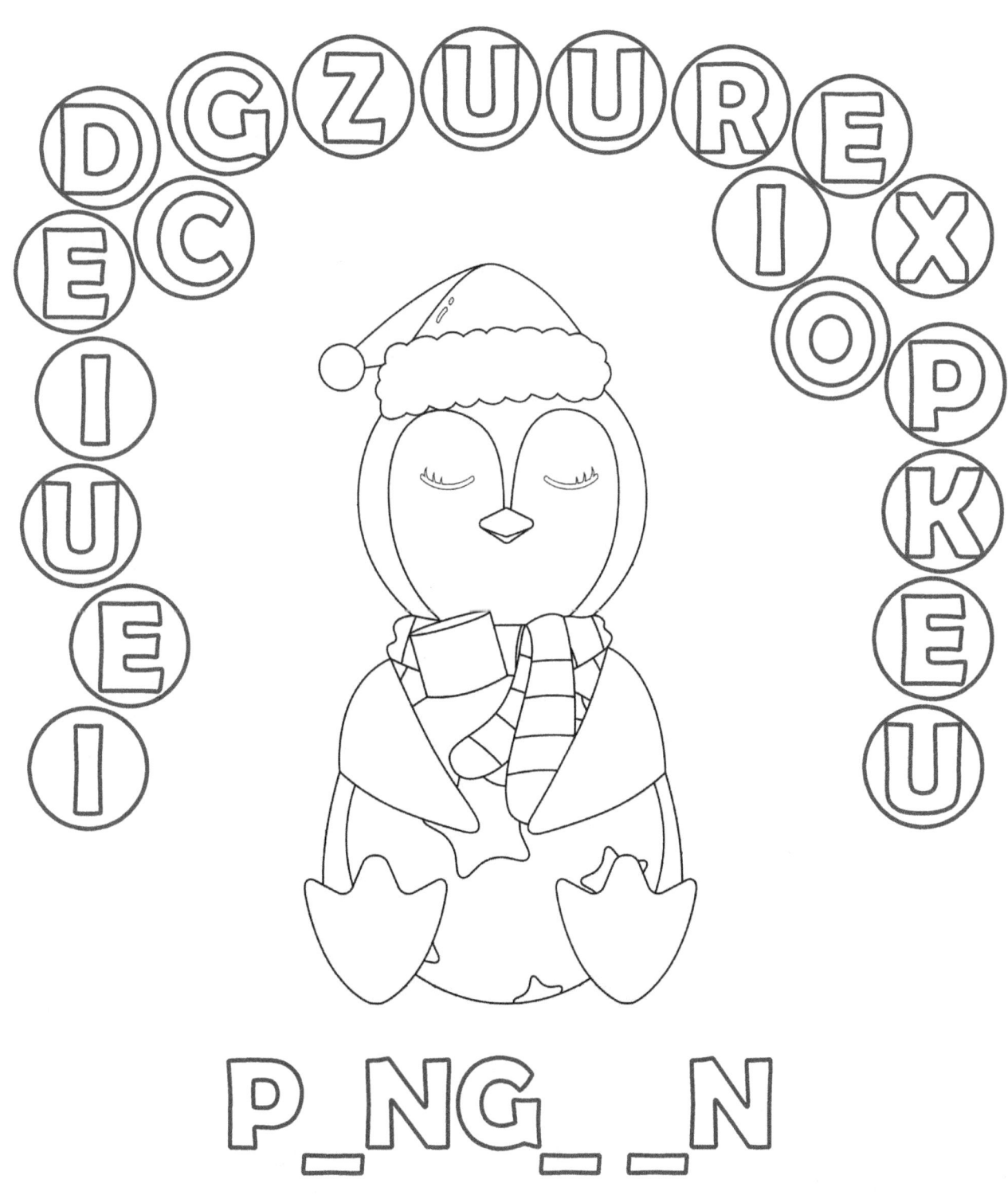

P_NG__N

Find, color, and write the missing letters

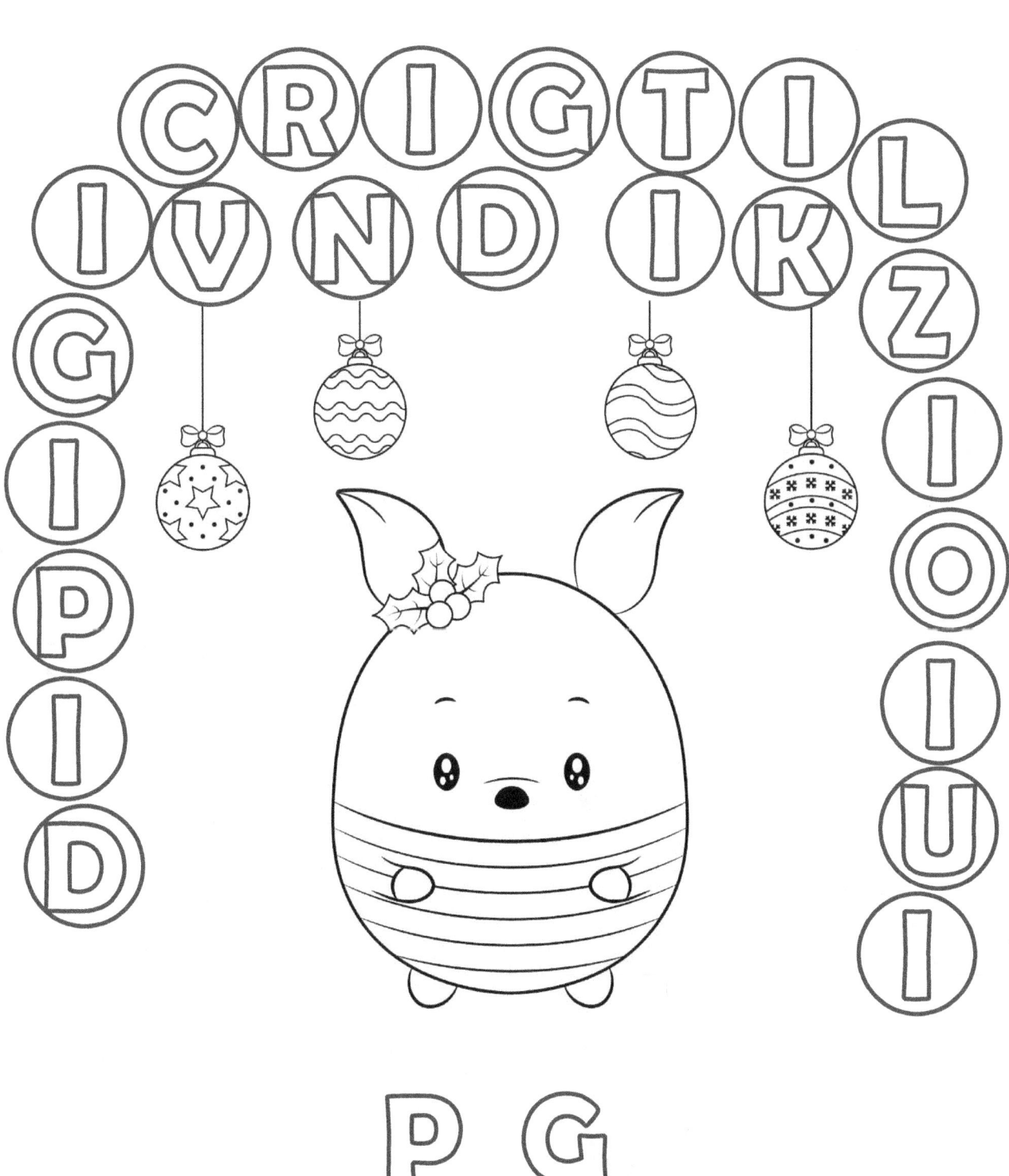

P_G

Find, color, and write the missing letters

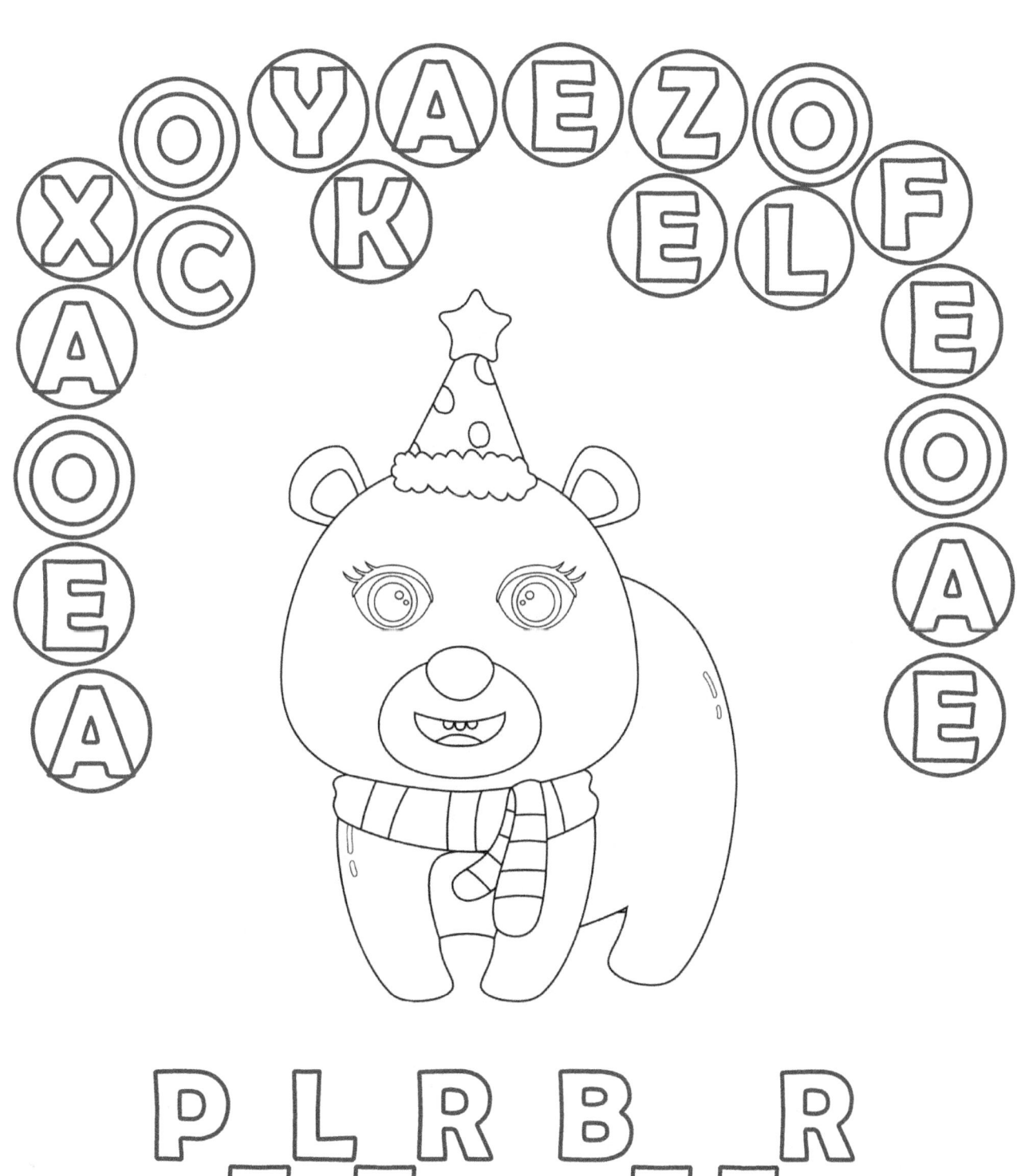

P _ L _ R   B _ _ R

Find, color, and write the missing letters

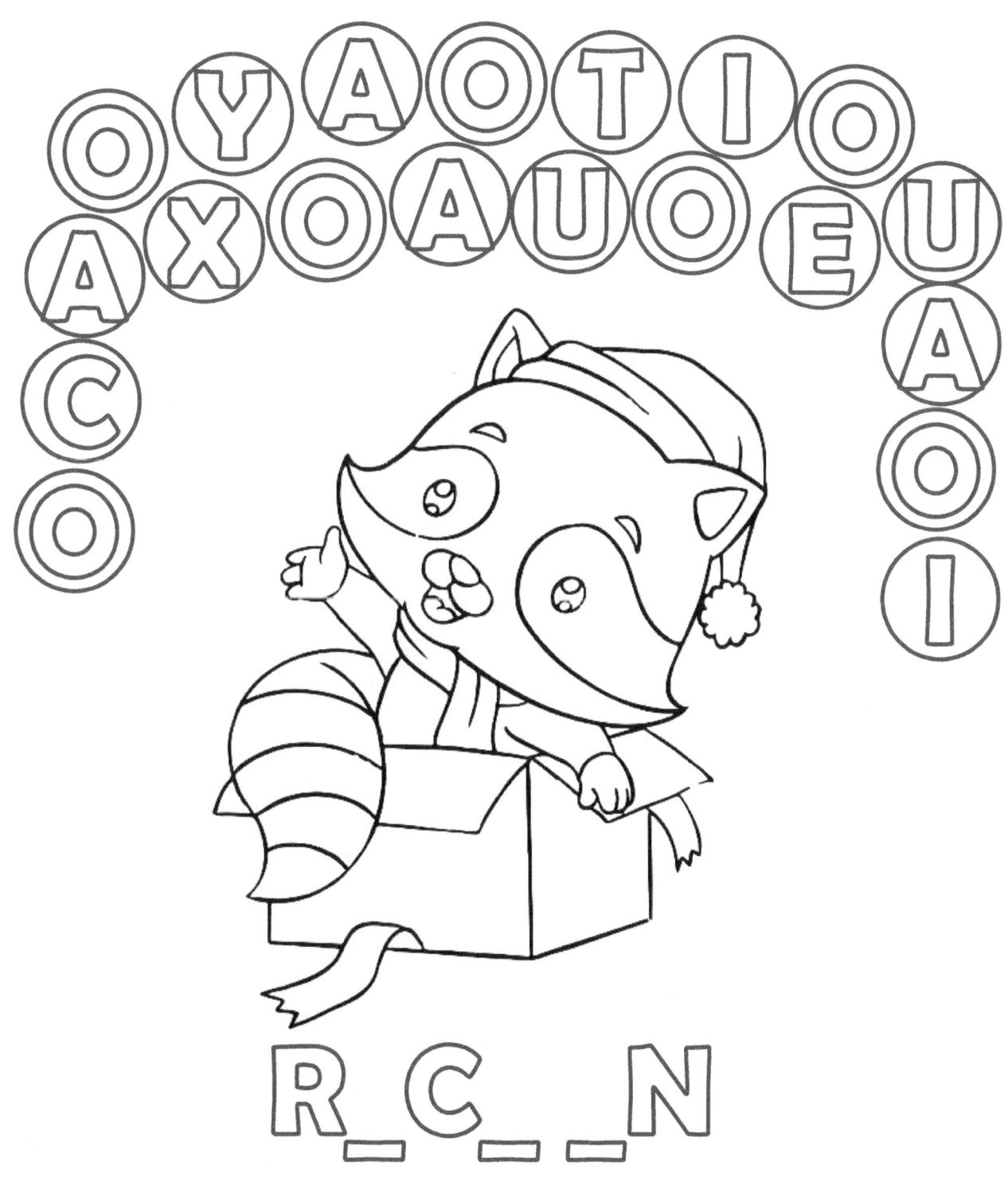

R _ C _ _ N

Find, color, and write the missing letters

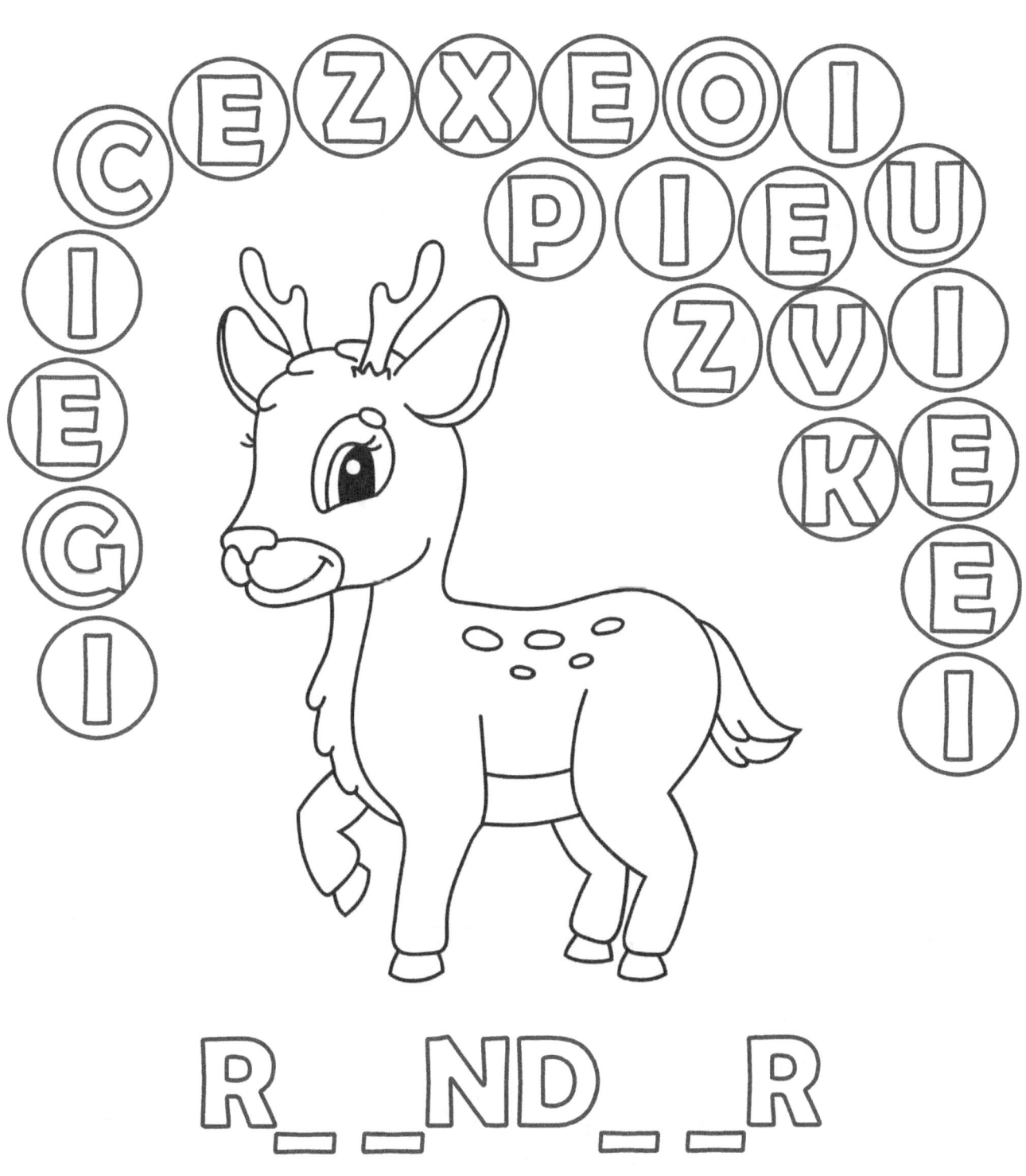

R _ _ N D _ _ R

Find, color, and write the missing letters

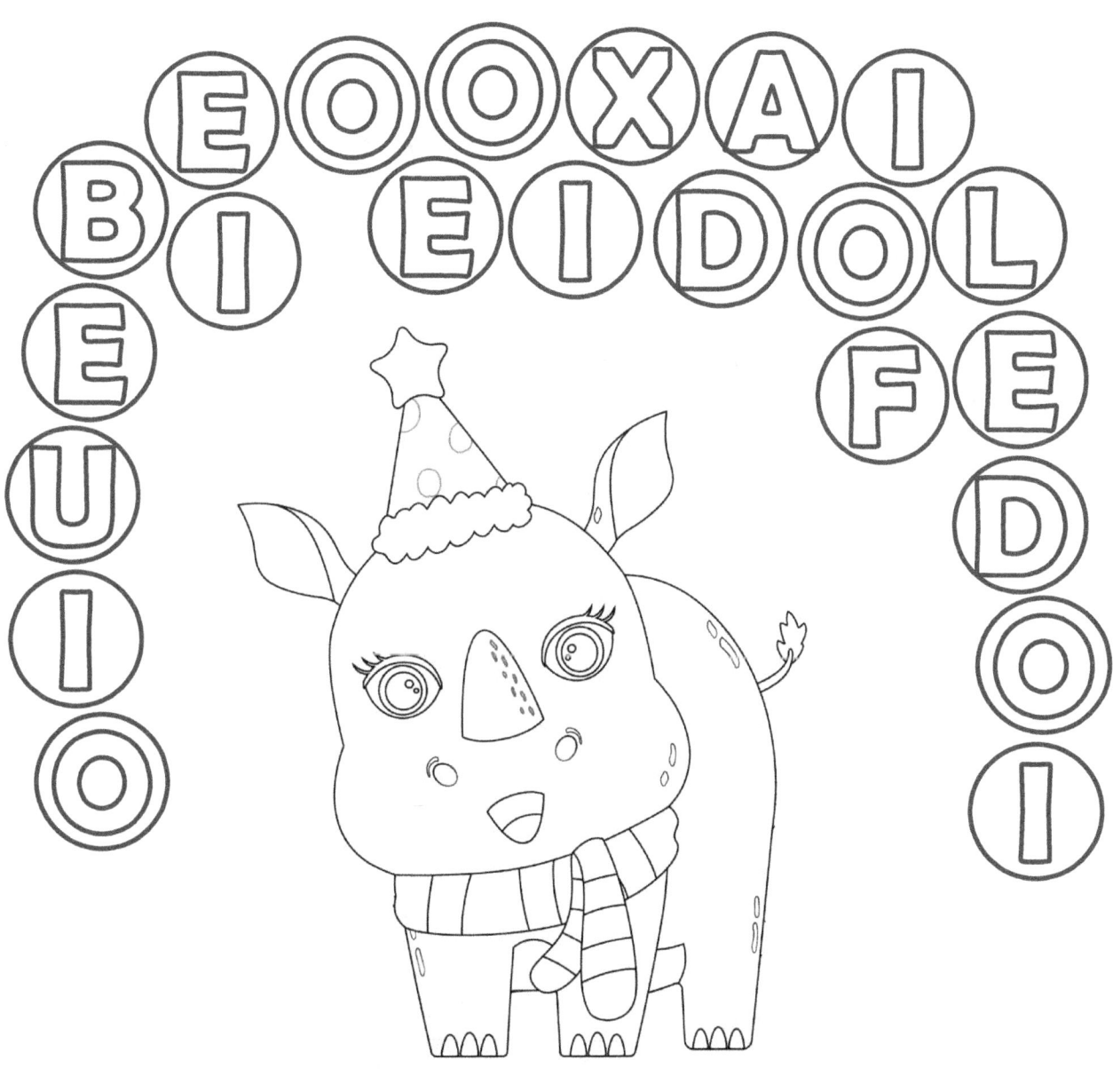

RH_N_C_R_NS

Find, color, and write the missing letters

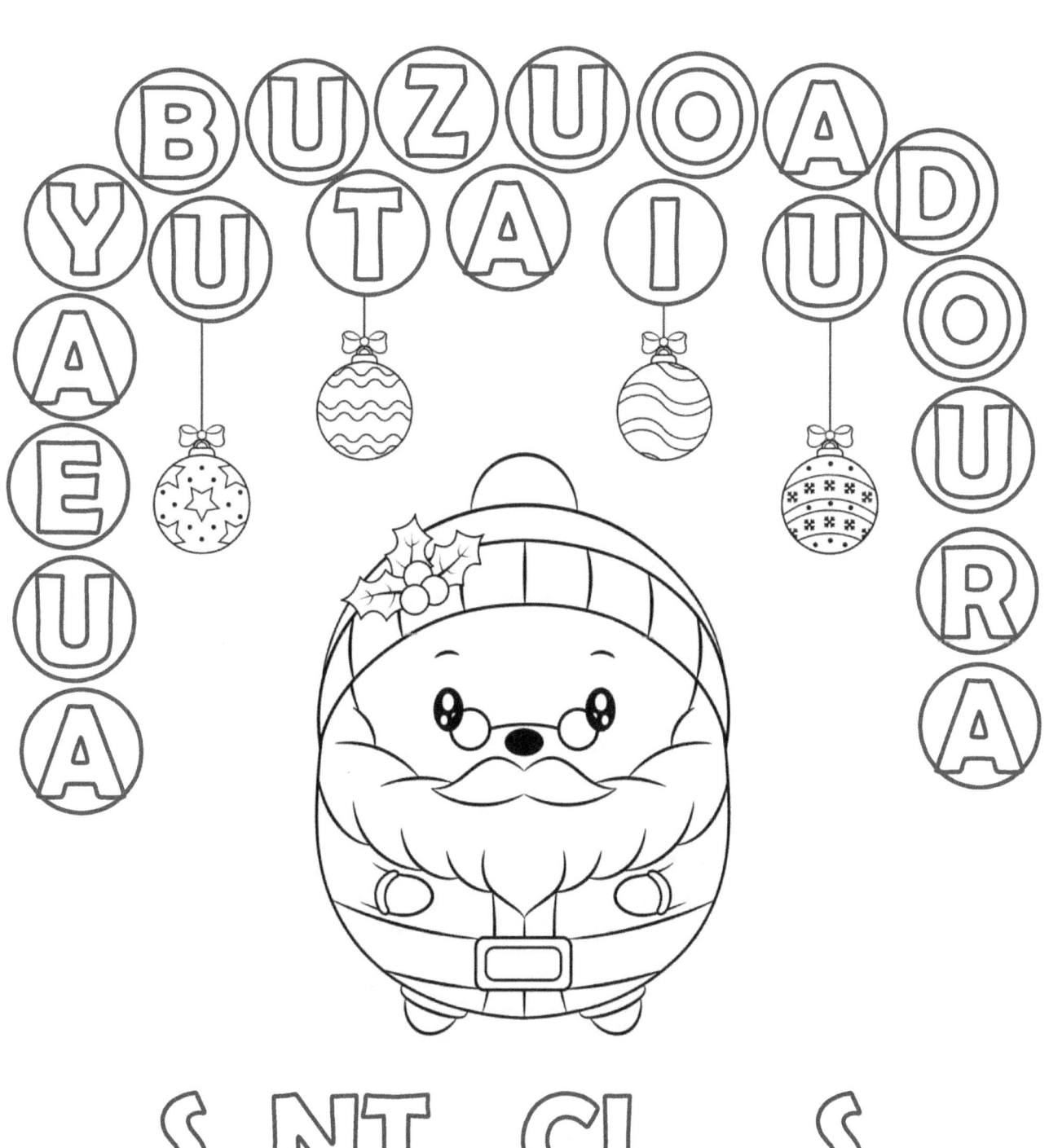

S_NT_ CL_ _S

Find, color, and write the missing letters

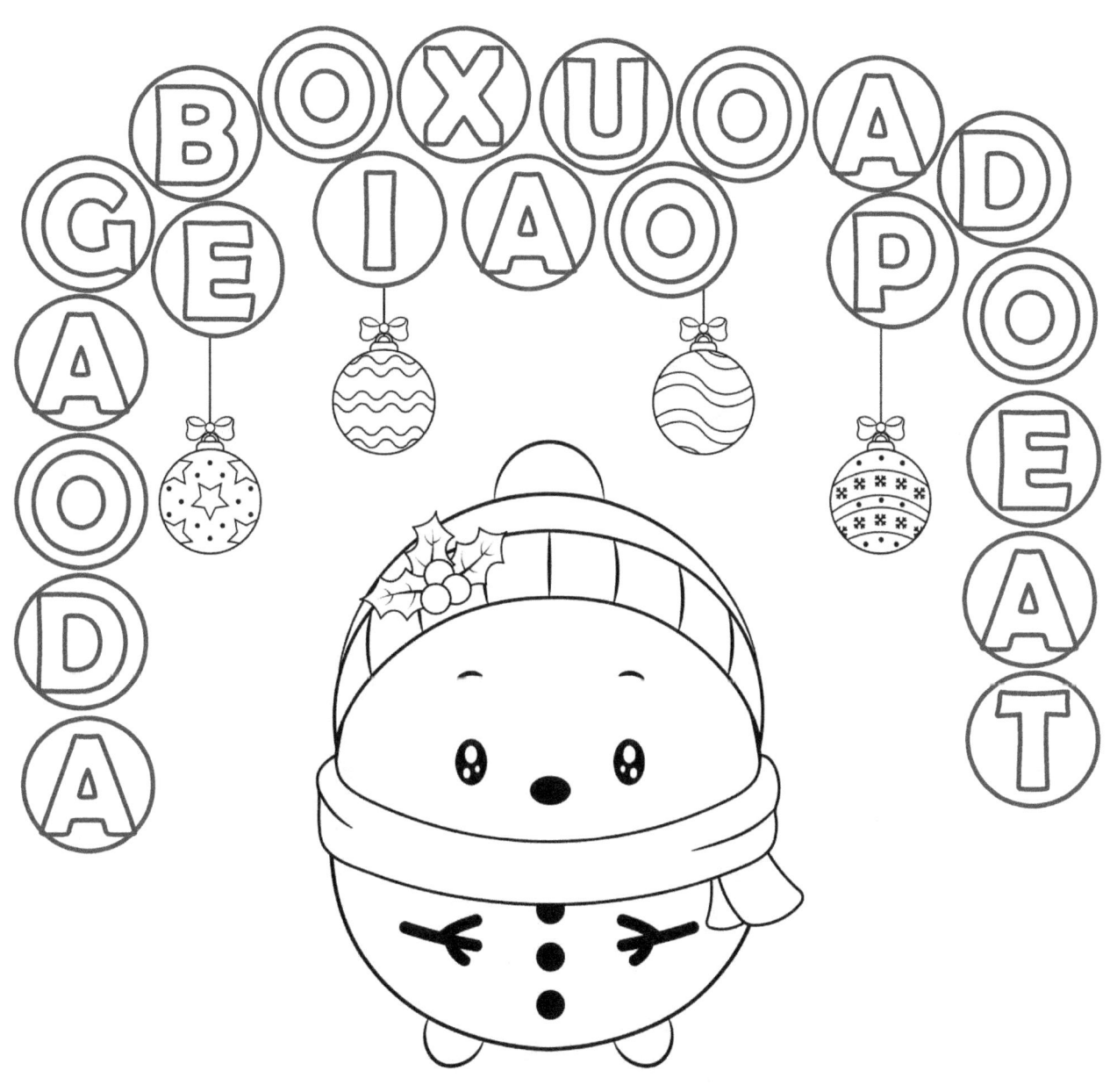

SN_WM_N

Find, color, and write the missing letters

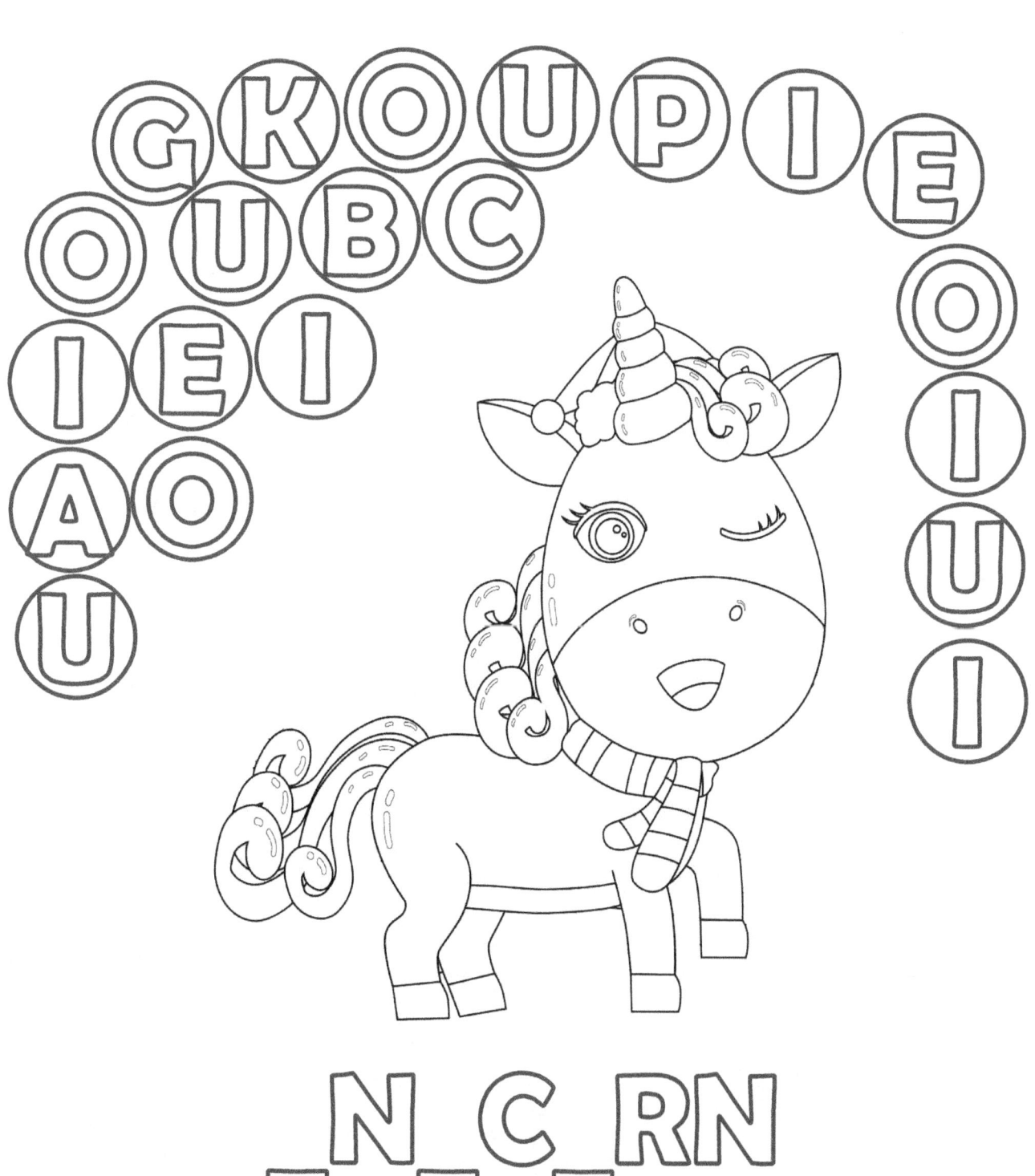

_ N _ C _ RN

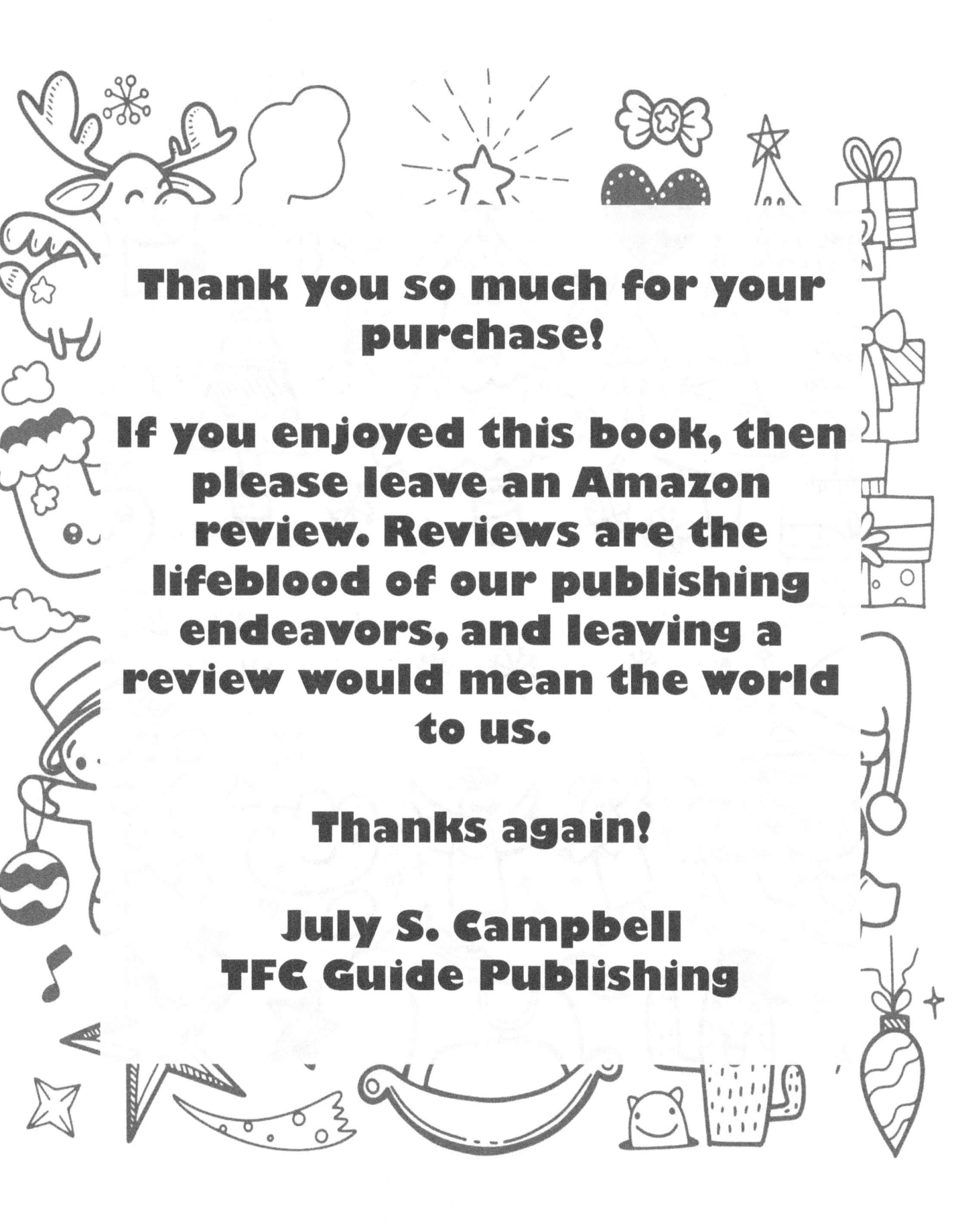

Thank you so much for your purchase!

If you enjoyed this book, then please leave an Amazon review. Reviews are the lifeblood of our publishing endeavors, and leaving a review would mean the world to us.

Thanks again!

July S. Campbell
TFC Guide Publishing

JUST A QUICK FAVOR...

Please feel free to send us any comments or suggestions through the following channels:

Email: admin@tfcguide.com

Please write to us, and we will send you digital templates as a gift.

Our goal is to improve and create more valuable books for you. Thanks again!

July S. Campbell
TFC Guide Publishing

Available now on Amazon

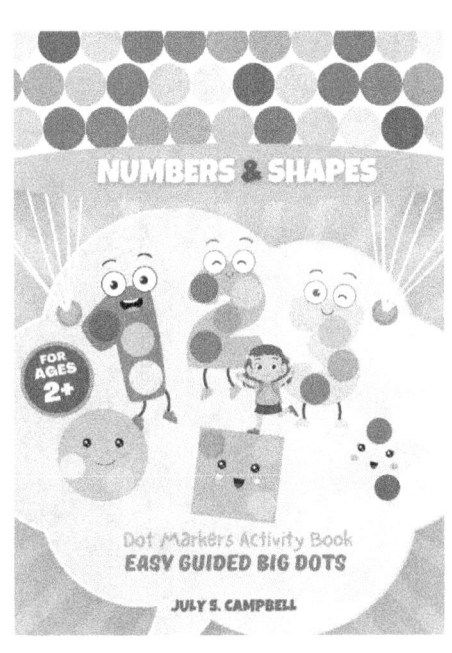

★★★★★

PAPERBACK ASIN: B08LJXP83B

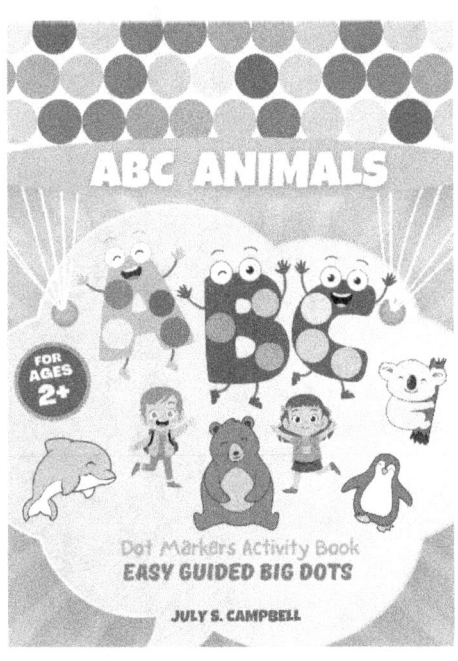

★★★★★

PAPERBACK ASIN: B08LNJJB7C

More books by July S. Campbell

SCAN ME